WHAT OTHERS ARE SAYIN

Alistair Petrie has unlocked and highlighted many subtle problems and issues that are facing the Church today. The profound insights, when put into action, will empower the Church to establish God's Kingdom. *God's Design For Challenging Times*, should become required reading for every leader in the Body of Christ. May God stir us all to action!

Rev. Dr Naomi Dowdy
Founder, TCA College, Singapore
Former Senior Pastor, Trinity Christian Centre, Singapore
Author, International Speaker/Trainer

In every generation God summons some of His servants to be "watchmen". They stand on the wall, see what is coming, hear the word of the Lord, and alert the people of God. In *God's Design For Challenging Times*, Alistair Petrie is fulfilling this ancient commission with a wake–up call that we as a Church must heed! This very important book—based on painstaking research and bathed in diligent prayer—it will realign your thinking and priorities and prepare you for the season of shaking *and glory* in the days ahead.

Steven Fry
President, The Messenger Fellowship, Nashville, USA

If you are looking for more understanding about the times in which we live, if you are longing to be better equipped for prayer and action in your community/nation, then this masterly book is for you! Drawing on many years of experience and his deep love of Scripture, Alistair's profound insights offer essential foundations for following God's ways through these challenging times.

Jane Holloway
National Prayer Director, World Prayer Centre, Birmingham, UK

Awesome book! A true wake–up call for Christians. Alistair Petrie helps to bring a spiritual plumb line into every aspect of our lives. God desires to see His Kingdom established on the Earth. Are you looking for a breakthrough in your business, your church, your city or your community? Read this book and discover how God wants to partner with you to pray strategically to remove those barriers preventing you from fulfilling God's vision.

Greg Simpson
President/CEO, Simpson Seeds Inc

Perhaps you, like many, have been blessed with the ministry of the Word through someone who later teaches things that don't "settle" right and leaves you questioning what happened and what is right. Many of these leaders are well–known and accepted by the church, so this only adds to the weight of the questions within. If so, you must read *God's Design For Challenging Times*. In Alistair's latest book, he shares Scriptural truths that provide answers with clarity. It is evident that it comes from someone who has gone through pain and paid a price to discover these truths. Truth that God's people so desperately need in order to protect themselves from deception in this most challenging hour in the history of mankind.

Dr Ruth J. Ruibal
International Conference Speaker, Author
Co–Founder and Senior Pastor, Ekklesía Centro Cristiano Colombiano
Cali, Colombia

GOD'S DESIGN FOR CHALLENGING TIMES

Discovering Freedom in
an Age of Compromise

Guidance For The Perplexed!

by

Rev. Dr Alistair Petrie

CHI-Books
PO Box 6462,
Upper Mt Gravatt, QLD 4122, Australia

www.chibooks.org
publisher@chibooks.org

God's Design For Challenging Times
Discovering Freedom in an Age of Compromise

Print edition ISBN 978-0-9870891-0-6
eBook edition ISBN 978-0-9870891-1-3

Other versions used as noted in endnotes are:

Amplified Bible (AMP), Published by The Lockman Foundation, 1987 Printing version as used on Bible Gateway; www.biblegateway.com

Complete Jewish Bible translated by David H Stern, Jewish New Testament Publications, Inc., Clarksville, Maryland USA, 1998. ISBN: 0 19 529751 2.

Common English Bible, (CEB), 2011, Bible Gateway – www.biblegateway.com

Good News Translation (GNT), 1966, 1971, 1976, American Bible Society – ISBN: 08883 40427.

Holman Christian Standard Bible (HCSB) 1999, 2000, 2002, 2003, 2009 by Holman Bible Publishers, Nashville, Tennessee (Source – http://www.biblegateway.com)

Life Application Bible – Tyndale House Publishers Ind., Wheaton, Il 60189 July 1988 – ISBN: 0 8423 2551 4.

New American Standard Version (NASV); The Lockman Foundation; 1995 Printing as used on Bible Gateway Website www.revival-library.org

The New English Bible (NEB), New York, Oxford University Press, 1971.

Printed in Australia, United Kingdom and the United States of America.

Distributed in the USA and Internationally by Ingram Book Group and Amazon.

Editorial assistance: Anne Hamilton

Cover design: Dave Stone

Layout: Jonathan Gould

CONTENTS

ACKNOWLEDGEMENTS

Upon the completion of a project such as this book, I find there is much to reflect upon. So many people – family – friends – Board members – colleagues – have encouraged me to complete this work since it represents a journey that has had many challenges.

In particular, I want to thank my wife Marie, our sons Mike and Richard, and their wives, Anna and Dama, for allowing me the time and space needed to complete this project. Their prayers and advice and insights have been of immense help.

If I thanked everyone involved in this process, the list would be endless — but I do want to cite those that have had significant input into my life other than my family. Ruth, Sheryl, Ray, Peter, Mary, Lorrie, Steve, Margaret, David, Lance, Jill and Bob! You are amazing friends and colleagues.

Special thanks to Errol and Helen who have walked with us for over 30 years and a special thanks to Jim and Jeannie Rodgers — especially to Jeannie for typing and retyping the manuscript!

Most of all — thanks to our Lord Jesus Christ who has patiently been with me step by step. It's been quite the journey. May He receive all the honour and glory that may come from these pages in the days that lie ahead.

DEDICATION

I am not old, but I am growing older. I am perhaps more aware of the brevity of time than I have been in earlier years. I want to ensure that I do fulfill the purpose for which God formed and fashioned me. I am also aware of the importance of legacy and what we hand on to the generations that follow us until the Return of Jesus Christ.

I have always had a curious nature which probably can be discerned from the contents of this and earlier books. But it is with fascination I note that some of my curiosity has been passed on to my grandchildren. I enjoy watching them as they grow and develop each in their own unique way. At this time of writing, Marie and I have three grandsons and one further grandchild on the way. It is to them that I dedicate this book.

On one occasion, I was reading through the Book of Proverbs, and I came upon a verse that caught my full attention. The first part of Proverbs 13:22 simply states "A good man leaves an inheritance for his children's children..." Simple — yet profound! It's all about grandparents and grandchildren!

We love and serve the God of all generations. Scripture is clear on generational legacy. As I was writing this book there were many occasions when I felt like stopping the project since it has not been without its challenges and interruptions. Yet time and time again I felt the nudging of the Holy Spirit that I had to complete this work since it was important for my grandchildren — why?

The pages of this book offer a blueprint for helping in navigating the years that lie ahead before the Return of the Lord. Clearly, it would appear as if the countdown has begun. There will be increasing issues and events in these coming days that will attempt to distract the people of God from what is at hand. I realize more than ever the importance of depositing into my grandchildren all that the Lord has given me. This is part of the inheritance God has given me that is to be shared with those that follow. This book is part of that inheritance and my prayer is that it will enable my grandchildren to walk in the fullness of their calling without compromise.

So Elijah, Daniel, Benjamin and whatever other grandchildren I may have yet to enter this world, I dedicate this book to you — it will soon be time for you to pick up the baton, and to run the race with perseverance that has been marked out for you. May the pages of this book help you on that journey.

Go for it — and keep your eyes fixed on Jesus, the Author and Perfecter of our faith.

With love, prayers, and blessings,
Grandpa

Alistair P. Petrie (Kelowna, BC, 2013)

FOREWORD

Truth and freedom are two sides of the same coin. You cannot experience the sort of freedom that Jesus talked about in John 8:32 without first knowing the truth and applying it in your life as a disciple. The key to freedom is simply knowing the truth and applying it in one's life.

In the days when the boy Samuel was called to be a prophet, the Scripture tells us that *"the word of the Lord was rare; there were not many visions"* (1 Samuel 3:1). And the prophet Amos talks about days when the Lord would *"send a famine through the land — not a famine of food or a thirst for water, but a famine of hearing the words of the Lord"* (Amos 8:11).

The days in which we are living are similar to the days of Samuel or Amos. It is an age when all moral boundaries have disappeared from society and when there are myriad discordant voices inside the Body of Christ, often teaching things which seem to be at variance with the solid foundations of understanding that Scripture provides. In these days, we desperately need to know who is speaking truth into today's Church — and speaking it with an integrity that is unquestionable, in an era of compromise that is littered with false and deceptive teaching.

For this very reason I feel very privileged to have been asked to write the *Foreword* to one of the most important books that has appeared for many years. It comes from the pen of a writer who has not only studied the signs of the times, but has searched and re–searched like no–one else I know, for what God is seeking to say to His people. His writing is backed up with an unquestionable commitment to Scriptural integrity.

For many years now I have had the joy of working with Alistair and Marie Petrie on schools and conferences in different parts of the world. And throughout all those years I have been constantly impacted by Alistair's extraordinary grasp of what is happening in the world and his ability to bring the searchlight of Scripture to bear on situation after situation.

The students on our own schools are amazed at the way Alistair unpacks complicated subjects and makes them relevant and understandable. He is able to chart a way through the religious jungle and lay a diamond–studded pathway of understanding, reflecting the light of truth into hearts and minds.

When, towards the end of His earthly ministry, the disciples asked Jesus about the signs of the end of the age, his reply was an eye–opener for both them and us, *"Watch out that no–one deceives you"* (Matthew 24:4). In such days, we all need teachers who will help us to recognise what is true and avoid the traps of deception. Alistair Petrie is one of those.

Alistair tells us, *"This book is all about God's boundaries."* That gladdens my heart for, in my own experience of ministering to many thousands of people over the past thirty years, the largest single reason I have discovered why people get themselves into a personal mess is because they have ignored the boundaries that God has laid down for his people.

God's boundaries are parameters of safety. They are, indeed, the manifestation of God's amazing grace. They are not for discussion or negotiation — they are simply there to accept and live within. For, as Alistair says, *"when we determine to live life in the way He intended, this leads to the abundant life promised in John 10:10 and Romans 5:17."*

We need to rediscover these boundaries of God — sadly, for many people, they are like old, disused railway tracks, covered over with weeds and barely recognizable. The purpose of a track is to guide the train to its destination. This book will help you remove the weeds and get back on track and, I pray, help you reach a destination of understanding about some of the most vital and relevant issues that currently prevail in today's church. I will be strongly recommending it to all the students who come on our courses and schools. It's life–changing.

Peter Horrobin

Founder and International Director of
Ellel Ministries International www.ellelministries.org

INTRODUCTION

DIVINE DRAMA IN OUR MIDST

September 11th, 2001 is a date that will be forever etched in human history. It was a watershed moment that will never be forgotten. I vividly recall where I was at that moment. My wife and I were returning from a series of conferences in Australia, and we were airborne while the terrorist strikes were taking place. Several aircraft had been warned that they could be carrying terrorists. We were on one of the very few aircraft where much of the developing drama was being shared with the passengers. The Captain came and talked to a few of us in the area where we were seated. He was highly concerned—as were the rest of us once we were told what was happening. I turned around to my wife and I recall saying, "Honey, things will never be the same again."

At that exact moment something happened to me personally that I will never forget. It was as if the physical voice of God quickly cited five distinct issues that would forever change my life in ministry. I referenced this event in the introduction of our book, *Transformed! People — Cities — Nations*[1], but never specifically referred to what God so clearly placed on my heart and, which in the weeks that followed, had an increasing effect upon me. These five issues were as follows:

- This is the end of the age of innocence
- This is a wake–up call to the church

- You are now seeing a glimpse of the spiritual realm on the physical realm (a new spiritual grid)
- This is the beginning of the age of compromise and deception—things will never be the same again
- Don't preach and teach the same way again!—*every moment counts!*

Some months later my wife and I were meeting with a few other leaders in a residential retreat. As we sought the Lord on the events that had been taking place in these months since 9–11, He seemed to impress upon us all that He was giving the Church a ten year period of preparation before He would raise the curtain on what these developing "end times" would look like. In other words, as leaders, we felt there was to be a ten year period of preparation during which the Church had to become properly prepared and positioned for the final days before the return of Christ.

Exactly ten years later on September 11th, 2011, I was the guest preacher at a church in Atlantic Canada. As I was sharing my message, the Lord suddenly spoke into my spirit and said that this ten year period had been fulfilled, and that now the curtain was about to be raised on the next stage of His divine drama. As He quickened my spirit I was immediately made aware of many events during the previous 10 years and understood their relevance for a time such as this. I was sharing my message, but He was clearly placing His message deep within me on this significant date. God had my undivided attention! There was movement in the heavenlies! A "Divine shift" was occurring.

When we originally founded Partnership Ministries, part of the mandate we believed God placed upon us was to be an "Issachar" ministry—understanding the signs of the times. Our mission statement states we combine prayer and research that prepares communities, cities, nations and the marketplace for lasting revival, authentic transformation and the release of Kingdom culture. Since 2001, I have observed many communities and cities enter into what is termed community transformation—which, by definition, simply means the fabric of an entire community or city begins to reflect the presence and glory of God in a manner that can be evaluated and compared over previous years. Yet at the same time the last few years have disclosed many issues within the global arena that previously had concealed corruption and deception. Consider, for example, the documentary distributed by Sony Pictures entitled *Inside Job*[2]. This very insightful documentary concerning the global economic crisis of 2008 went on to win the 2011 Academy Award for documentaries. Imagine winning an Academy Award for revealing deception and corruption within the economic arena! Several other such documentaries have also been released in the last few years. This is a testimony to the times in which we live. It is as if we live in an era in which previously hidden issues at all levels of life are now being exposed, and that we need to have an understanding in these matters, from God's point of view! It is as if God Himself is giving us the answer to a question many are asking—"What, on earth, is going on in the world, for Heaven's sake?" We are living in challenging times and in an age of compromise, but if we learn to navigate what lies ahead with His roadmap and understand what is at stake, we will receive His direction and discover the freedom of knowing He is ultimately in charge!

I believe we are living in a time of increasing lawlessness and entitlement.

LAWLESSNESS AND ENTITLEMENT

I believe we are living in a time of increasing lawlessness and entitlement. Humanity as a whole tends to embrace an ever increasing principle of independence—which in effect is just a return to Genesis 11. Here, in Scripture, we find what may be cited as the four pillars of humanism. Simply put, these four pillars are:

Come — we will make bricks (*creation*)

Come — we will build a city (*development*)

Come — we will build a tower to the heavens (*self–rule*)

Come — we will make a name for ourselves (*destiny*)

Both inside and outside the church at large, we seem to be experiencing an increase in lawlessness—which simply means people are doing whatever they please and whatever they choose in their own way. They live without reference to any particular standard (least of all one given by the living God). Let's recall what we learn in Genesis 3. Here, again in Scripture, we find what can be termed as the four pillars of paganism:

You will not die

Your eyes will be opened (wisdom/knowledge) (the third eye)—it will be pleasing…

You will be like God

You will know good and evil.

John puts it very succinctly in his epistle, 1 John 3:4, *"Everyone who sins breaks the law; in fact, sin is lawlessness."* Concerning the man of lawlessness referred to by Paul in 2 Thessalonians 2:3–4, *"Don't let anyone deceive you in any way, for that day will not come, until the rebellion occurs and the man of lawlessness is revealed, the man doomed to destruction. He will oppose and exalt himself over everything that is called God or his worship, so that he sets himself up in God's temple, proclaiming himself to be God."* Paul further adds in the first part of verse 7—*"for the secret power of lawlessness is already at work."*

> Lawlessness and entitlement is simply man imposing his own ideals and standards upon every world system arising from his pride, arrogance and a total disregard of God.

Feeding upon this lawlessness is the appeal towards entitlement which means every one of us on the planet earth has the right to appropriate and achieve and receive whatever we choose. Both lawlessness and entitlement are spirits rooted in the spirit of Baalism—the spirit of

Nimrod which is the foundation of Genesis Chapter 11. The issues of self–rule—pride—control—sexuality—money—and so on, all find their roots in this spiritual system. However, all of 2 Thessalonians needs to be understood especially in terms in what happened in Genesis 11 and the effect this has had upon subsequent generations right up to this very day.

Lawlessness and entitlement is simply man imposing his own ideals and standards upon every world system arising from his pride, arrogance and a total disregard of God. It is a form of Luciferianism which influences man's thinking and action, in which the individual determines the standards of life based on humanism and relativism. Both of these are born out of deism and dualism which began to shape the thinking of the emerging church after the fourth century AD.

In the chapters that follow, the release of the era of deception as referred to in Scripture, especially in the end times, will be described. In these end times, lawlessness and entitlement will feed both relativism and a lifestyle without restraints or restrictions. In other words, all God–given boundaries as revealed in Scripture will be removed.

LAWLESSNESS HAS CONSEQUENCES

Railroad crossing signs exist for a reason: they warn us to be cautious before crossing a set of railway tracks! Yet at times I have seen vehicles speeding across the tracks as the drivers try to beat an approaching train. They ignore all the warning bells and flashing lights. While mechanical error can account for some fatal encounters between trains and automobiles, human error is often the problem. People just simply ignore the signs. They feel they know better and then suffer the consequences. One website gives a very sobering account of the number of train incidents that have taken place globally in the last few years. In February 2012, a passenger train in Canada derailed injuring dozens of people. Three engineers died in the accident simply because the safety precautions for speed restriction were not maintained.

In another incident on January 13th, 2012, the *Costa Concordia* cruise ship was sailing a few hundred meters off the rocky Tuscan coastline.

Near the island of Giglio, it went off course and consequently ran on to rocks. This horrific navigational accident cost the lives of many people and the loss of a massive cruise liner. It was a mistake caused by a deliberate human decision to change from the set course. This incident shook the cruise line industry to its core and brought immense embarrassment upon the nation of Italy. Had some key laws of navigation not been ignored, this tragedy would never have occurred.

Over the years our ministry has conducted seminars and conferences in many nations. Frequently I have been asked to give an update on the signs of the times. Using Scripture as a "divine filter", it is not too difficult to decipher what God is saying to the world in this day and age. He uses familiar issues in order to get our attention: finance, economy, weather, natural events, political issues, as well as moral, ethical and spiritual matters.

God is clearly giving indicators to His people to alert us to the times in which we live. He is shaking the systems of the world. He is trying to get our attention. We are living in the end times—even though no one knows specifically when Jesus Christ will return for His church. However, in these remaining years during which the great commission will be fulfilled, God has given to His people strategic warning signs of the times, to keep us on course for what He has called us to do before the return of Jesus Christ.

This book is all about God's boundaries. He has given us parameters and safety measures that will release His protection, His provision, His direction and even His correction in our lives. These are non-negotiable principles that affect us at a personal level, a family level, a church level, a business level, a city level, a regional level and even at a national level.

Whether we choose to look at the news on the web, on television, in newspapers or in periodicals, it is not hard to realize that we are living in serious times. God is revealing the depth of deception that is occurring at many different levels as society breaks or compromises the boundaries He has set. We can expect that one divine disclosure after another will take place in the coming years. Divine drama is all around us on an ever–increasing basis. If we ignore the increasing signs of the times, it will be at our peril. As I have travelled, I have noticed that God tends to shake an individual or a city or a nation when His boundary lines of life are ignored, broken or changed. My wife and I recently were talking about the contents of this book and in the course of conversation when discussing the theme, I simply said, "Well, in the end, it's all about boundaries." This is not a negative or limiting subject which so often is the interpretation of the word "boundaries". Rather, it is an engaging and liberating subject when we understand why God has given to His people boundary lines and boundary stones. We are all on a journey at this time—let's not ignore the warning lights and signs en route. May the eyes of our hearts be opened and filled with fresh understanding.

---

1. *Transformed! People–Cities–Nations* Author: Alistair P. Petrie Republished July 2008 – Sovereign World Ltd – ISBN 97818 52404 826
2. *Inside Job* DVD Video – Sony Pictures Classics – Directed by Charles Ferguson

1

GOD'S REDEMPTIVE *Shakings*

As I travel I am often asked if it is God who is shaking the systems of the world, or is He simply using current ecological and economic events to His advantage as part of as strategic wake–up call—or perhaps a combination of both? Whatever the response may be, there is a growing assumption that God is trying to get our attention! Indeed, many biblical passages describe what is often referred to as the "end times". In Luke 21:25–26 we are given a highly serious warning —*"There will be signs in the sun, moon and stars. On the earth, nations will be in anguish and perplexity at the roaring and tossing of the sea. Men will faint from terror, apprehensive of what is coming on the world, for the heavenly bodies will be shaken."* When reference is being made to God shaking the world, it is essential that we examine this within the context of Scripture.

Haggai 2:4–9 in the NASB[1] version: *"'But now take courage, Zerubbabel,' declares the LORD, 'take courage also, Joshua son of Jehozadak, the high priest, and all you people of the land take courage,' declares the LORD, 'and work; for I am with you,' declares the LORD of hosts. 'As for the promise which I made you when you came out of Egypt, My Spirit is abiding in your midst; do not fear!' For thus says the* Lord *of hosts, ' Once more in a little while, I am going to shake the heavens and the earth, the sea also and the dry land. I will shake all the nations; and they will come with the wealth of all nations, and I will fill this house with glory,' says the* Lord *of hosts. 'The silver is Mine and the gold is Mine,' declares the* Lord *of hosts. 'The latter glory of this house will be greater than the former,' says the* Lord *of hosts, 'and in this place I shall give peace,' declares the* Lord *of hosts."* Then in the first part of verse 22, God says quite clearly—*"I will overthrow the thrones of kingdoms and destroy the power of the kingdoms of the nations."*

The prophet Haggai was raised up by God to encourage the Jews in the rebuilding of the temple (Ezra 5:1–2; Haggai 1:1). Haggai challenged the leaders and the people of Judah from their spiritual lethargy in order to encourage them to continue working on the temple. As is often the case with Old Testament biblical prophecy, there is both a present and a future component. While people are being encouraged and exhorted to rebuild the temple of the day, God was also referring to the future glory of the millennial temple and the future glory that this implied. This passage also indicates that part of God's character is to intervene in the lives of His people and at times this could be in the form of supernatural and ecological events.

Turning to Hebrews 12:26–28 NASB, we read these words—*"And His voice shook the earth then, but now He has promised, saying, "Yet once more I will shake not only the earth, but also the heaven." This expression, "Yet once more," denotes the removing of those things which can be shaken, as of created things, so that those things which cannot be shaken may remain. Therefore, since we receive a kingdom which cannot be shaken, let us show gratitude, by which we may offer to God an acceptable service with reverence and awe."*

If we examine these two passages of Scripture carefully, we will see God's activity in five different areas:

He is ***shaking*** the earth!
He is ***shaking*** the heavens!
He is ***shaking*** the sea!

He is ***shaking*** the land!
He is ***shaking*** the kingdoms of nations!

Whenever God speaks in this manner, we need to realize it is a **wake–up call** to His people. When framed within the context of biblical prophecy, it is the all–knowing, and all–seeing God who is in fact giving His people adequate warning concerning the future. He does this so that we, as His people, will not be afraid. He does it also so that we will be fully awake, aware, ready and prepared for what He is doing in our midst and what will develop in the days that lie ahead.

Ponder the words found in Matthew 24:29–30—*"...the sun will be darkened and the moon will not give its light; the stars will fall from the sky and the heavenly bodies will be shaken. At that time the sign of the son of man will appear in the sky, and all the nations of the earth will mourn. They will see the son of man coming on the clouds of the sky, with power and great glory."*

If we take this passage within the full context of Matthew 24 alongside the parallel passages found in Mark 13 and Luke 21, we will find a significant and alarming list of signs of the "end times" which can readily be framed within the subject of "divine shakings". These signs include:

Wars and rumors of wars
Uprisings and revolutions
Earthquakes
Natural disasters
Lawlessness
False prophets
False teachers
False messiahs
The rise of previously unimaginable evil in our culture
Persecution of Christians
Betrayal
Apostasy
And so the list goes on...

Some proponents of extreme dominion theology would state that subsequent to the fall of Jerusalem in AD 70, these and other passages within the New Testament were all fulfilled—which points towards a postmillennial position that suggests once every city and nation has acknowledged Jesus Christ as Lord then He will return. I do not readily agree with that line of thinking since, from a research perspective, the wake–up signs in these passages are significantly on the increase. Along with the relentless rise of these signs, the majority of cities and nations seem to be increasingly distancing themselves from Christianity.

HOW DO WE RESPOND TO THIS?

This is a very challenging question since, if we were to collate all the conditions occurring in different societies before an authentic move of God occurs, we can look upon the past and present situation with sobriety, challenge, and yet with high level expectation.

The Revival Library website[2] (www.revival–library.org) refers to comments made by J. Edwin Orr concerning life in the 18th Century, prior to the Great Awakening. There was a profound moral slump in the wake of the American Revolution. Profanity was rampant and social dishevelment could be seen at all levels of society. It was not safe for women to be out by themselves at night, banks were robbed almost on a daily basis, churches were rapidly losing membership—and even clergy were seeking other forms of employment. Few students within the US Educational system at that time would admit to being part of the Christian faith.

J. Edwin Orr observed that the situation was changed only through a concert of prayer. He referred to Jonathan Edwards who just before the 1734 revival in North Hampton said, "We have reason to fear that our iniquities, our coldness in religion, and the general carnality of our spirits, have raised a wall of separation between God and us: and we may add, the pride and perverse humor of infidelity, degeneracy and apostasy from the Christian faith, which have of late years broken out against us, seem to have provoked the Spirit of Christ to absent himself much from our nation. Return oh Lord, and visit thy church and receive thine own work in the midst of us." (Quote taken from Revival Library

Website[3] entitled "Conditions That Require Revival")

This same social backdrop of drunkenness, degeneracy, sexual impropriety, profanity, lawlessness and a general disregard for God were common denominators throughout all the major historical revivals including the Welsh and the Hebrides revivals. Over the years our research into historical Revival has proven this to be the case. In itself, it has become an essential catalysis of desperation which ignited corporate, tenacious prayer and a fresh dependence upon God for a change in the seeming hopelessness of the hour.

Because of his very nature, God cannot and will not permit spiritual decline to continue unchecked.

As Arthur Wallis writes in his book, *In the Day of Thy Power*[4] first published in 1956—"...there is an element of judgement present in every revival. The purifying and the quickening of the people of God are moral and spiritual necessities. Because of his very nature, God cannot and will not permit spiritual decline to continue unchecked. He is ever halting and reversing the trend of the times by means of revival—or judgement. Where His people are not prepared for the one, they shut themselves up to the other." It would certainly seem that whatever we sow, whether on a personal or a corporate level, ultimately we reap as a consequential harvest.

Charles Finney once made a sobering point that can be applied throughout hundreds of years of biblical history. "The fact is that Christians are more to blame for not being revived, than sinners are for not being converted."[5] He goes on to say: "How often God visited the Jewish church with judgements because they would not repent and be revived at the call of his prophets! Churches and whole denominations are cursed with a curse, because they would not wake up and seek the Lord and pray..." Finney also said, "Without revival, shame will cover the church more and more until everyone holds the church in

Pillars of Awareness

contempt."[6] His thesis is that without revival the church will decline into oblivion.

Over the years I have worked with several communities that have experienced God's transforming power. One such recent example is found in the community of Manchester, Eastern Kentucky. The Sentinel Group produced an excellent documentary on the move of God in that community entitled *An Appalachian Dawn.*[7] One of the community leaders, Pastor Doug Abner, shares these challenging words on the DVD, "Good people sat back and did nothing, and I'm convinced that's a big part of our problem. We talk about how bad the darkness was but the lack of light was more of a problem than the darkness."

The good news in all this is that God patiently reminds us of what has happened in history in order to alert us to our present circumstances and prepare us for the future. The sobering fact is that time is running out. We have to be about the business of preparing ourselves, our communities and cities, and our nations for what could be the final move of God before the return of His Son.

Pillars of Awareness

Throughout history certain indicators emerge which are wake–up calls before a coming move of God. I refer to these as "the pillars of awareness".

The **first pillar** represents the simultaneous shaking of the Church, the government and business. When these three components are being refined and purified so as to determine what is and what is not of God, we should take careful note.

The **second pillar** of awareness is when God shakes the four ancient elements—wind, fire, water and land.

There is a distinct relationship between the four elements, issues on the land, and God's intervention in the ebb and flow of humanity as described in *Releasing Heaven On Earth.*[8] A brief synopsis would be as follows:

- The land contains the product of blessing and curse of previous years and generations;
- This becomes a *"feeding trough"* for whatever takes place on this property in both present and future generations;
- Until the present–day stewards address issues—*issues from the past*—they can still be an integral part of a spiritual "cause–and–effect", which can lead to various forms of malaise;
- Until these issues are addressed the "product" is subject to robbery, exploitation, usury and to whatever else may be in opposition to God's purpose for His people;
- This, in turn, releases a significant cause–and–effect on the ability of executing the vision of the organization (church, city, nation) and its productivity;
- The **land** represents "God's opinion" of things!

If we examine the "intense shaking" in the Scriptures we have reviewed so far from Haggai 2:6–9, Hebrews 12:25–28 and Matthew 24, we see it can be itemized in at least five specific areas.

1. Spiritual systems (corruption within the church)
2. Economic systems (corruption within industry and commerce)
3. Political systems (corruption within government and politics)
4. Communication and technology (corruption within the power of media)
5. Personal lifestyles (corruption in ethics, morals, motivations—no regard for God)

Putting it another way, whatever is hidden and secret is being exposed and brought to the light. As even a casual glance at the news on a daily basis indicates, horrifying agendas are now out in the open revealing the extent of high level corruption in nations, governmental systems, cities, businesses and enterprises—even in the church.

WHAT DOES THIS MEAN?

Here are just a few examples that help to explain what has just been cited:

> Ecologically speaking, many of the costliest and most expensive hurricanes in US history have occurred since 9/11. While hurricane Katrina devastated New Orleans resulting in a loss of $108 Billion, Hurricane Sandy devastated the Eastern coast in late October, 2012. The Investopedia.com website[9] cites comments made by Eqecat, a catastrophic risk management consulting firm, which estimates the actual damage caused by the storm was between $30–$50 Billion, with insurance companies being liable for amounts up to $20B.
>
> In 2011, the US suffered the worst outbreak of tornadoes in almost 50 years.
>
> In March 2011 a devastating earthquake hit the area of Sendai in Japan which moved the entire island eight feet!
>
> The rotation of the earth on its axis has continued to slow down over the last several years.
>
> The earth's axis has shifted by almost 6.5 inches in recent history. Experts suggest this is due to the pummeling of earthquakes, tsunamis and experimental nuclear explosions upon the surface of the earth.
>
> The dust storms that affected Australia in 2009 displaced 75,000 tonnes of dirt every hour for 48 hours which, experts say, will require up to 300 years for the soil to be replenished.
>
> Weather patterns globally are completely bewildering according to meteorologists. Hardly anything is definitive any longer and unusual weather is affecting tourism. One article in *The Atlantic Wire*[10] on Friday July 6th, 2012 read as follows: "...you can't sue God or Mother Nature, so Belgian tourist officials want to do the next best thing: sue the people who forecast the weather." However, are the extreme weather shifts that are now experienced globally really the fault of weather forecasters?

In October, 2012 an Italian Court convicted 6 scientists and a government official for failing to predict the 6.3 earthquake on April 6th 2009 that killed 300 people. Negligence and malpractice were cited in their evaluation of the danger of an earthquake and subsequently not correctly informing people of the risks. One wonders if the fear of litigation may deter scientists from working on averting future earthquakes.

On July 10th 2012, *The Guardian*[11] newspaper released the following headline—"Scientists attribute extreme weather to man-made climate change." The article explains that climate change researchers now believe they can attribute various examples of extreme weather conditions to the effects of human activity on the planet's climate systems. While the article gives various examples of this research, in the end does it not simply come down to a relationship between God and man, with man being held responsible for his stewardship upon the planet earth?

In his book, *Lectures on Revival,*[12] Charles Finney makes a fascinating comment that one may expect Revival—"When the providence of God—His ordering of events—signals an awakening is at hand... God shows His will in many ways—sometimes by giving unusually effective tools or methods, sometimes by alarming events, *by the weather* (emphasis mine), health, and so on."

In the area of environment, wildlife experts have noted an unprecedented level of fatalities involving animals, birds, fish and sea life. Even honey bees, strategic in various areas of agriculture, have experienced massive death rates. Again, even while logical explanations are given by experts, other experts give contradictory opinions and say no one really knows why these extraordinary occurrences are taking place all over the world.

In the area of economics and finance, things are precarious, putting it mildly. On October 9th, 2008, the US national debt was $9,536,317,663,429 or over nine trillion dollars. Debt is now one of the main commodities in the USA. At the time of writing this book, according to the US Congressional budget office, the US federal debt had risen in excess of 16 trillion dollars, with a potential debt of $30 trillion looming within the next decade. Some economic experts predict this to be as high as $50 trillion but, whatever the actual amount, debt is rising exponentially in the US and this trend is not likely to change in the foreseeable future

Mathematicians have calculated that, if the US paid $1.00 each second to reduce its national debt, it would take more than 32,000 years to pay off just one of those trillion dollars!

The bankruptcy of nations is moving from potentiality to reality, as seen in Italy, Greece, Iceland, Ireland, Portugal, Spain and Hungary. In the UK, *The Independent* newspaper printed this headline—"Treasury prepares for financial Armageddon." The newspaper went on to indicate that the UK has now been given a "heads up" for what the business secretary calls an "Armageddon scenario" (quote from *The Independent* Newspaper[13], November 11th, 2011). The *Daily Mail*[14] Newspaper in the UK had this headline on November 10th, 2011—"Staring into the Abyss". The article indicated that Italy's economy was in crisis, France was under strain and there were fears that Britain could be dragged into a second recession... with the economic contagion claiming Italy as its biggest victim, leaving Europe facing a "lost decade" of financial chaos.

Thousands of banks have closed globally since 2008. The term "fundless banks" has been used to describe the utter chaos within present–day financial markets. Some banks are so desperately looking for money that, at times, they offer a reduction on owed principal if they are promised an early mortgage payout! Undeniably, debt has grown globally to a crisis level. The majority of many western governments are now spending well beyond their means. We are at the point in the global economic arena when there will likely be a fully–fledged debt write–down that will bring on a fully–fledged depression. It may well be that governments will just simply print more money for bail–outs of the banks, causing hyperinflation.

Perhaps it is time to review the sobering warning found in Haggai Chapter 1:8–11. Part of this passage states—*"You expected much, but see, it turned out to be little. What you brought home, I blew away. Why?" declares the Lord Almighty. "Because of my house, which remains a ruin, while each of you is busy with his own house. Therefore, because of you the heavens have withheld their dew and the earth its crops. I called for a drought on the fields and the mountains, on the grain, the new wine, the oil and whatever the ground produces, on men and cattle, and on the labor of your hands."* No wonder the people responded accordingly and obeyed and feared the voice of the Lord (v12).

Is this to be our response for today? If we are indeed in the countdown before the return of Jesus Christ, is this what Malachi 3:2–3 is indicating—*"...who can endure the day of His coming? Who can stand when He appears? For He will be like a refiner's fire or a launderer's soap. He will sit as a refiner and purifier of silver...then the Lord will have men who will bring offerings in righteousness..."*

Economic issues are forcing the introduction of criminal categories never seen before. On July 1st, 2011, the Bribery Act of 2010 came into force in the UK. The act established that it was an offence for commercial organizations to fail to prevent bribery. Shortly before the introduction of the Act the government published its adequate Procedures Act Guidance. This set out six procedural principles required to prevent bribery and to encourage whistle–blowing procedures in order to minimize corruption in the business realm. It is quite amazing to realize that we now live in an era in which bribes have formed part of our economic structure. Any form of corruption, be it financial or political, is a real detriment to the wealth/health of a nation.

Our next point concerns culture, morality and ethics. Web search engines continually cite statistics on Christianity and diminishing moral standards in society. According to a 2006 article written by Jerry Ropelato[15] on a Google Pornography Statistics Site, the pornography industry was larger than the revenues of Microsoft, Google, Amazon, eBay, Yahoo, Apple and Netflix combined. These statistics have increased

> There is a growing disconnect between those who identify as Christians, and their "salt and light" witness in society.

alarmingly since then! Sexual liberty is now trumping religious liberty in the USA. Concerned social service and ministry organizations indicate the global child sex slavery trade has reached an overwhelming level. Meanwhile, when we consider the on–going debate over abortion, Wikipedia cites a statistic from the Centers of Disease Control (CDC) that since 1973 at which time the Supreme Court set guidelines for the availability of abortion, approximately 50 million legally induced abortions have been performed in the USA.

On another highly debated subject, same sex marriages have become acceptable in several Christian denominations. Divorce statistics are similar, whether marriages are conducted inside or outside the

church. There is a growing disconnect between those who identify as Christians, and their "salt and light" witness in society.

The Barna Group under the direction of George Barna[16] gives regular updates on a variety of subjects affecting both the church and the global arena. In a combination of research statistics, the Barna group indicates:

- Only 9% of professing Christians in the USA have a biblical worldview yet 85% of Americans identify themselves as Christian.
- 84% of Christians view the Bible as a holy or sacred book, only 56% believe it is accurate and without error.
- Only 40% of Christians believe Satan is real, while 46% hold to absolute moral truth.
- Only 62% believe Jesus was sinless while as of 2011, the research indicated that 25% of American Christians now subscribe to universalism.

Book: The Harbinger 2011

If indeed the church is a sign of the kingdom of God and even a litmus test of society, then we are in serious days. It is little wonder that the Refiner is shaking His church with divine fervor! If the church is indeed the prophetic mouthpiece for society and we are either marginalizing ourselves or straying far from the perimeters of authentic and biblical authority, then we might well ask what on earth is being proclaimed from the mouth of the church in this day and age! No wonder God is allowing both the world and the church to go through a serious time of shaking. Undoubtedly He is fulfilling the words of Haggai—*"I will overthrow the thrones of kingdoms and destroy the power of the kingdoms of the nations."*

God is allowing both the world and the church to go through a serious time of shaking.

It is not purely circumstantial that Jonathan Cahn released his bestseller *The Harbinger*[17] in 2011. In this book Cahn offers not only a prophetic message holding certain secrets for the future of America but also an understanding of the current global collapse. *"Before its end as a nation, there appeared in ancient Israel a series of specific omens and signs warning of destruction—these same Nine Harbingers are now manifesting in America with profound ramifications for America's future and end–time prophecy."*[18]

In light in what we have seen so far, let us review present–day circumstances in the framework of these questions:

- Is God shaking us?
- Is He punishing us?
- Is He trying to get our attention?
- Does He want to refine and purify us?

We can summarize what we have seen and respond to these questions when we consider them in the context of "God's redemptive shakings". If God is who He says He is in Scripture, then these present–day shakings enable us to see reality from His perspective. Isaiah 32:3–4 puts it this way—*"And the eyes of those who see will no longer be closed, and the ears of those who hear will listen. The mind of the rash will know and understand, and the stammering tongue will be fluent and clear."*

1 Samuel 2:6–8 also give some graphic insight on this whole subject, *"The LORD brings death and makes alive; he brings down to the grave and raises up. The LORD sends poverty and wealth; he humbles and he exalts. He raises the poor from the dust and lifts the needy from the ash heap; he seats them with princes and has them inherit a throne of honor. 'For the foundations of the earth are the LORD's; on them he has set the world.'"* If the people of God are going to be praying with realistic insight and any degree of tangible authority, then we have to be informed about the issues causing these redemptive shakings at this time. We need to have all our "fantasy thinking" removed (a phrase I first heard used by Mary Glazier of Windwalkers International[19] based in Alaska).

God is shaking us because He is reminding us that the earth is His and so are the people who dwell upon the earth. (Psalm 24:1) All the world systems and structures ultimately come under His authority. This is so, even if we do not choose to believe that principle either for the life of the individual or for the nation.

He is shaking us because He loves us and wants us to repent.

He is shaking us because He is indicating that we are running in the opposite direction from Him but it is not too late! We have to *turn around.* He wants to forgive us and restore us to a place of intimacy and fellowship with Him.

He is shaking us so that we let go of anything prohibiting or impeding our relationship with Him. This includes any form of ideology, philosophy, religious belief, political belief system or even possessions—indeed anything that gives a sense of false peace and security…anything that seduces us away from our intimacy with Him…anything that creates a spiritual anaesthesia over His people.

He is shaking us so that we will know that there is no true peace or security except what is made available through Jesus Christ. In the words of Jesus Himself—*"Peace I leave with you; my peace I give you. I do not give to you as the world gives. Do not let your hearts be troubled and do not be afraid."* (John 14:27) He goes on to say, *"I have told you these things so that in me you may have peace. In this world you will have trouble. But take heart! I have overcome the world."* (John 16:33)

He is shaking us because He has a mission for His church and He is reminding us that we are His prophetic mouthpiece.

He is shaking us because He has a mission for His church and He is reminding us that we are His prophetic mouthpiece and therefore, we are His sign of the Kingdom of God in society today. This was the challenge faced by Jonah. His "ship of escape" consequently entered a huge time of shaking, and it was then the captain (synonymous with the head of secular life) told him to stop sleeping on the job and to call upon his God! Amazing—even secular leadership was telling Jonah (symbolizing the leadership of his day) to get into the place of his calling, otherwise everyone would perish! Just think about it, a pagan ship captain had to shake a teacher of God's Word, wake him up and beg him to pray for his salvation. This is a sobering message for anyone who believes they are part of the body of Christ!

He is shaking us to purify us, to discipline us, to prepare us and to qualify us for all that lies ahead in what will probably be the greatest moment in biblical history— the countdown for the return of Jesus Christ, the bridegroom of the Church.

He is shaking us because time is running out, and Jesus is coming back soon. This is now the moment God has given us to put into alignment with Him things that are currently out of alignment. Titus 2:14 states clearly that He is purifying for Himself a people that are his very own.

God's redemptive shakings are all about His being at work in the world systems and structures, shaking everyone—everything, everywhere, removing what is not of Him and establishing and confirming what is of Him.

Scripture is quite clear on this point— *"...all the foundations of the earth are shaken."* Whatever is not of God is now being exposed. In this vein, Matthew 24:29–30 would imply that the powers of the heavens will be shaken, and all spiritual systems that affect the physical systems of life today are being brought into the light.

Why does it seem that God is allowing this shaking to take place today? The answer comes with a challenging reminder—He permits it so as to separate the sheep from the goats. (Matthew 25:32)

My family comes from a farming background and, as many farmers will indicate, sheep tend to cluster together and heed their shepherd, while goats can be very indifferent and wayward except when it comes to feeding time! The gospel of the kingdom of God is the power unto salvation (Matthew 24:14) and, in the end, this present–day shaking can only solidify and confirm our position in Christ knowing that the kingdom of God in us can never be shaken.

Putting it very simply, God's redemptive shakings are all about His being at work in the world systems and structures, shaking everyone—everything, everywhere, removing what is not of Him and establishing and confirming what is of Him. Acts 17:28 reminds us: *"For in Him we live and move and have our being. ...We are His offspring."* Similarly, Colossians 3:3 indicates, *"For you died, and your life is now hidden with Christ in God."* Colossians 1:27 gives us a profound assurance— *"...to them God has chosen to make known among the Gentiles the glorious riches of this mystery which is Christ in you, the hope of glory."* This is why the psalmist could say with assurance—*"He alone is my rock and my salvation; he is my fortress, I will never be shaken."* (Psalm 62:2) The Life Application Bible[20] translates these words with a sense of confirmation—*"Yes, He alone is my Rock, my rescuer, defence and fortress. Why then should I be tense with fear when troubles come?"*

We are clearly told not to develop a false security or dependency upon anyone or anything else other than the Father.

In reality, there is little point in asking God *not* to shake us, because quite simply it is in His will and power to do so! (Psalm 115:3 reminds us: *"Our God is in heaven; He does whatever pleases Him."*) As we have been learning in this chapter, only the things that cannot be shaken will be left.

So in summary, what is God shaking in this day age with His divine and redemptive initiative?

- Empires
- Nations
- Governments
- Monarchies
- Banking and all money and financial systems
- Businesses
- Churches and all denominational systems
- Families
- Individuals
- And anything else that is not eternal!

As Mark 4:22 reminds us, *"For whatever is hidden is meant to be disclosed, and whatever is concealed is meant to be brought out into the open."*

Concerning who we are as the body of Christ, Matthew 5:14–16 reminds us, *"You are the light of the world. A city on a hill cannot be hidden... let your light shine before men, that they may see your good deeds and praise your Father in heaven."* As 1 John 2:15–17 would indicate, we are clearly told not to develop a false security or dependency upon anyone or anything else other than the Father, since *"...The world and its desires pass away, but the man who does the will of God lives forever."*

CLARIFYING WHO IS THE POTTER AND WHO IS THE CLAY!

We may not realize it at first, but it is God fighting for His people through these redemptive shakings out of His deep *chesed*[*] love for us—determining who are of Him and who are not. As we have already seen, ever since the four pillars of paganism in Genesis 3 and the four pillars of humanism in Genesis 11, mankind has fought with these distinctive foes that would attempt to negate the intimacy and dependency of our relationship upon God. No wonder Isaiah 45:9–12 makes this sobering observation—*"Woe to him who quarrels with his Maker, to him who is but a potsherd among the potsherds on the ground. Does the clay say to the potter, 'What are you making?' Does your work say, 'He has no hands'? Woe to him who says to his father, 'What have you begotten?' or to his mother, 'What have you brought to birth?' This is what the LORD says—the Holy One of Israel, and its Maker: Concerning things to come, do you question me about my children, or give me orders about the work of my hands? It is I who made the earth and created mankind upon it. My own hands stretched out the heavens; I marshaled their starry hosts."* Isaiah 64:8 puts it succinctly—*"Yet, O, LORD, you are our Father. We are the clay, you are the potter; we are all the work of your hand."*

God's word is very clear on this matter—*"...can I not do with you as this potter does?" declares the LORD. 'Like clay in the hand of the potter, so*

---

* This Hebrew word **chesed** can be translated by loving-kindness and mercy, used in the Psalms (23 times, plus Hosea 2:19) when it refers to God's love for His people Israel, yet we must always beware lest we think that God is content with less than righteousness. The word stands for the wonder of His unfailing love for the people of His choice and the solving of the problem of the relation between His righteousness and His loving-kindness passes beyond human comprehension. *www.bible-researcher.com/chesed.html*

are you in my hand, O house of Israel." (Jeremiah 18:6) We are created in the image of God, not God in our image!

God wants to clarify a key principle in the way that we operate as His church— *"Woe to those who call evil good and good evil, who put darkness for light and light for darkness, who put bitter for sweet and sweet for bitter. Woe to those who are wise in their own eyes and clever in their own sight."* (Isaiah 5:20–21)

Jeremiah 6:14 further states, *"They dress the wound of my people as though it were not serious. 'Peace, peace,' they say, when there is no peace."* Paul also clarifies this point in Romans 9:19–21, *"One of you will say to me: 'Then why does God still blame us? For who resists his will?' But who are you, O man, to talk back to God? Shall what is formed say to him who formed it, 'Why did you make me like this?' Does not the potter have the right to make out of the same lump of clay some pottery for noble purposes and some for common use?"*

Jesus put it this way in Matthew 5:37—*"Simply let your 'Yes' be 'Yes' and your 'No', 'No'; anything beyond this comes from the evil one."*

There is a reason why God is so clear on this issue of who we are in relationship to Him. This is a weighty statement from the Lord Himself— *"If at any time I announce that a nation or kingdom is to be uprooted, torn down and destroyed, and if that nation I warned repents of its evil, then I will relent and not inflict on it the disaster I had planned. And if at another time I announce that a nation or kingdom is to be built up and planted, and if it does evil in my sight and does not obey me, then I will reconsider the good I had intended to do for it."* (Jeremiah 18:7–10)

As we will see later in this book, it is when the people of God have ignored the boundaries, or parameters for living life in the way He designed for us, that we suffer the consequences. But when we determine to live life in the way He intended, this leads to the abundant life promised in John 10:10 and Romans 5:17.

Jesus gave a sobering warning to the church of Sardis in His revelation to John (Revelation 3:2–3). There were four key issues at stake here:

We should note that a common denominator of every authentic Awakening or Revival in history has been "repentance".

1. Wake up—open up your spiritual eyes to see things from God's perspective!
2. Strengthen what remains—don't forget your foundations—without them you will die. In other words, remember that He is the potter and we are the clay.
3. Remember what you have received and heard...there are rules and parameters for the type of life God wants us to live. The life we experience—and bear witness to—is meant to be from His perspective!
4. Obey the teaching and repent. We should note that a common denominator of every authentic Awakening or Revival in history has been "repentance".

What we have looked at so far is a summary of what God told His people would take place in the latter days before the return of Christ. It is a sobering wake–up call for a time such as this: one in which the clarity of God is increasingly apparent.

ISRAEL—FOR OR AGAINST?

God is also challenging the church of today in its attitude towards the subject of Israel.

Biblical prophecy makes it so clear that in the last days before the Second Coming, the whole world would witness the miraculous prophetic rebirth of Israel with the Jewish people returning to their homeland after centuries of exile. Modern history has shown us that this began in 1948 with the Jewish people beginning to rebuild the ancient ruins. Israel has increasingly become the epicenter of international attention as well as the thermometer by which we gauge the intensity and heat developing within the global arena. We are watching growing international hostility in the attitude of many nations concerning Israel. As a nation, it has become increasingly isolated in its relations with other nations. In reality, only a few nations acknowledge Israel's right to be a national sovereignty—an issue that will almost certainly intensify in the coming years.

This has all happened in our lifetime. This is what the ancients longed to see.

We can never fully understand the global arena and God's redemptive shakings without an understanding of Israel. The issue of Replacement Theology is a key challenge for a number of theologians and biblical scholars today. Many adamantly believe that the church has replaced Israel and is the recipient of all His divine favor and destiny. However, Israel will not go away!

We can never fully understand the global arena and God's redemptive shakings without an understanding of Israel.

There is a "divine" drama over Israel that is developing in this day and age, and it is not too hard to surmise that God is presently raising the curtain revealing a drama that has been going on for thousands of years. It could well be that this drama will find its conclusion in our lifetime. The subject of Israel will continue to gain momentum in the coming years. In fact, all that we have looked at in this chapter will undoubtedly continue to increase in a manner that will demand our attention, whether we like it or not.

SHAKEN—AND STIRRED!

Being shaken by God is, at times, very unpleasant. However through this discipline we will be purified and made ready to usher in the kingdom when He comes. As the writer to the Hebrews puts it succinctly—*"No discipline seems pleasant at the time, but painful. Later on, however, it produces a harvest of righteousness and peace for those who have been trained by it."* (Hebrews 12:11)

This is what divine strategy is all about. We are being purified and made ready for the return of Christ and as both Matthew 6:10 and Luke 11:2 state, it is all about the coming of His kingdom on earth. *"Your kingdom come, your will be done on earth as it is in heaven."* We read that Ruth and Naomi were preparing to enter their destiny as they approached Bethlehem and the whole town was stirred (Ruth 1:19). Similarly we, too, through this time of shaking, can be those used to stir *our* cities and nations into a time of preparation and awakening.

"Therefore, since we are receiving a kingdom that cannot be shaken, let us be thankful, and so worship God acceptably with reverence and awe, for our 'God is a consuming fire.'" (Hebrews 12:28–29)

DECEPTION IS KNOCKING AT THE DOOR

However, as part of this "shaking", God is challenging His Church on a non–negotiable issue. If we break or redefine the boundaries or parameters ***He*** has established for His people, then we can easily be led into a life of deception, and there is little doubt that we have now entered this era.

For many years I had puzzled over Matthew 24:24–25—*"For false Christs and false prophets will appear and perform great signs and miracles to deceive even the elect—if that were possible. See, I have told you ahead of time."* In the chapters that follow we are going to examine in some detail why we are living at such a critical moment in history. But we will also see why it is highly possible for even the elect to be deceived in this day and age!

---

1. *New American Standard Version*; The Lockman Foundation 1995 Printing as used on Bible Gateway Website www.biblegateway.com
2. www.revival–library.org
3. Ibid.
4. *In the Day of Thy Power* Author: Arthur Wallis – Christian Literature Crusade, 1956 (page 215)

5. *Lectures on Revival* Author: Charles G Finney – Bethany House Publishers, Minneapolis, Minnesota 55438, 1988 (Page 22) ISBN 1–55661–062–9
6. Ibid. (page 21)
7. *An Appalachian Dawn – 2010* TransformNations DVD Produced by The Sentinel Group ISBN 1–930612–33–8
8. *Releasing Heaven On Earth* Author: Alistair P. Petrie – Republished July 2008 – Sovereign World Ltd – ISBN 97818 52404 819
9. *Investopedia* Website – www.investopedia.com
10. *The Atlantic Wire* www.theatlanticwire.com
11. *The Guardian* www.guardian.co.uk
12. *Lectures on Revival* Author: Charles G Finney – Bethany House Publishers, Minneapolis, Minnesota 55438, 1988 (Page 23) ISBN 1–55661–062–9
13. *The Independent* www.independent.co.uk
14. *The Daily Mail* www.dailymail.co.uk
15. *Ropelato* – http://internet–filter–review.toptenreviews.com/internet–pornography–statistics.html
16. *George Barna* – www.barna.org
17. *The Harbinger* Author: Jonathan Cahn – 2011 – Published by FrontLine, Lake Mary, Florida 32746 ISBN 978 1 61638 610–8
18. *The Harbinger* Author: Jonathan Cahn – 2011 – Quote from back cover – Published by FrontLine, Lake Mary, Florida 32746 ISBN 978 1 61638 610–8
19. www.windwalkersinternational.org
20. *Life Application Bible* – Tyndale House Publishers Ind., Wheaton, Il 60189 July 1988 – ISBN 0 8423 2551 4

2

WHAT'S ALL THIS ABOUT *Deception?*

As we have now seen, the world as we know it is being shaken at virtually every level of life. We have seen Scripture repeatedly indicating there are consequences whenever God's parameters are broken. When the boundaries for life lived according to the kingdom of God are compromised, there are costs! As we will see in the chapters that follow, there are many reasons why God has established boundaries for His people. The words found in John 10:7–10 are key—*"Therefore Jesus said again, 'I tell you the truth, I am the gate for the sheep. All who ever came before me were thieves and robbers, but the sheep did not listen to them. I am the gate; whoever enters through me will be saved. He will come in and go out, and find pasture. The thief comes only to steal and kill and destroy; I have come that they may have life, and have it to the full.'"*

In Matthew 7:15–20, Jesus is warning his people to be on the lookout for false prophets who will come in sheep's clothing but who are, in reality, ferocious wolves. He warns us saying that it is by their fruit they will be recognized.

Later in 2 Thessalonians 2:9–12 Paul echoes a very similar warning. *"The coming of the lawless one will be in accordance with the work of Satan displayed in all kinds of counterfeit miracles, signs and wonders, and in every sort of evil that deceives those who are perishing. They perish because they refused to love the truth and so be saved. For this reason God sends them a powerful delusion so that they will believe the lie and so that all will be condemned who have not believed the truth but have delighted in wickedness."*

These passages contain sober warnings. Many years ago when I was training for the ministry, I spent one summer working with a company as a raspberry quality controller. This required my learning to look at the quality of raspberries, and to judge whether or not they were fit to be used in jam or yogurt. I had to look closely at all the berries and determine which ones had to be removed. I was in fact judging fruit! Fruit that did not meet a certain degree of quality was simply thrown away.

Paul makes an interesting comment in 1 Corinthians 5:12–13. He refers to the issue of 'judgement' and says quite clearly that we are to judge those inside the church before those outside the church. In fact, he says the latter is God's responsibility. This type of judging is in fact a form of fruit inspection!

OUR NATURE IS TO DECEIVE

As we have already seen in Genesis 3 and 11, humanity is subject to deception. Paul puts it very succinctly in Romans 3:23—*"For all have sinned and fall short of the glory of God,"* We are physically born into a world estranged from God, but through the work of Jesus Christ on the cross, we are redeemed and reconciled back into a relationship with Him. Paul explains the work of Christ in these profound words in 2 Corinthians 5:18–19—*"All this is from God, who reconciled us to himself through Christ and gave us the ministry of reconciliation: that God was reconciling the world to himself in Christ, not counting men's sins against them. And he has committed to us the message of reconciliation."* There has always been urgency on the part of the Godhead to bring mankind back into relationship with Himself—*"But God demonstrates his own love for us in this: While we were still sinners, Christ died for us."* (Romans 5:8)

This gift of reconciliation is not cheap! It cost God everything to make this possible for us through the death of His son. However, when we review Scripture we will see the depth of deception which is part of the result of our estrangement from God through the Fall as explained in Genesis 3.

Deception is sin, and sin, no matter how we justify it to ourselves, is often framed within deception.

JACOB'S DECEPTION OF ESAU

Genesis 27 gives a very vivid and detailed description of the power of deception. Disguising himself as Esau with a special type of garment, Jacob tricked Isaac his father. Isaac was visually impaired in his old age and Jacob pretended to be Esau. A gift of food and the smell of Esau's clothes overcame Isaac's doubts and he gave Jacob the blessing reserved for the firstborn—his older twin, Esau. When Esau returned, the act of deception came to the surface and the words of Isaac are penetrating—*"...Your brother came deceitfully and took your blessing."* (Genesis 27:35) Through this act of deception the brothers became estranged. Great sadness came to Isaac when he realized the manner in which his second–born had deceived him. Although this estrangement is addressed later on at a time when Esau literally runs to meet Jacob, embraces him, and forgives him (Genesis 33:1–4), nevertheless this passage clearly depicts the power of deception that so readily tries to remove us from our destiny.

Genesis 4:7 explains the result of the Fall that affects every one of us—*"If you do what is right, will you not be accepted? But if you do not do what is right, sin is crouching at your door; it desires to have you but you must master it."* The New English Bible[1] translation of this verse gives an even more somber warning—*"If you do well, you are accepted; if not, sin is a demon crouching at the door. It shall be eager for you, and you will be mastered by it."* Deception is sin, and sin, no matter how we justify it to ourselves, is often framed within deception.

HOW THE GIBEONITES DECEIVED JOSHUA

Joshua 9 is an eye–opening description concerning the power of deception. It also explains how the people of God can be deceived by the Deceiver, and how the enemy of God's people keeps busy laying his traps for us. Here we learn that the Gibeonites were afraid once they heard the reports of the defeat of the cities of Jericho and Ai. The way in which God had led His people to victory seriously frightened them. While the other kings came together to make war against Joshua and Israel (Joshua 9:2), instead the Gibeonites *"resorted to a ruse."* (Joshua 9:4) They pretended to come from a distant country. They gave the impression their city was from a far distance and was not part of the land God had promised the Israelites. They deceived Joshua by putting on old sandals and clothing and carrying moldy bread, saying that it had been fresh when they first made it at the beginning of their journey. They set out to deceive the Israelites in order to make a treaty of protection for themselves.

> Sin that is not properly addressed can have generational consequences! This is a huge spiritual principle that cannot be ignored.

Verse 14 is a significant warning—*"The men of Israel sampled their provisions but did not inquire of the Lord."* This was a huge mistake. Joshua made a treaty with these people, and he ratified it by an oath which in those days would not be broken. Perhaps a wake–up warning for us all is this, "Beware of those who come to us with worn out clothes and wineskins..." Or, putting it another way: prophecies and words and messages supposedly from the Lord that He never gave in the first place can easily penetrate our defenses if we do not ask the right questions and test their fruit!

Since the men of Israel had made a peace treaty with the Gibeonites they could not break the oath. In due course this affected both the

Gibeonites and the people of Israel. Joshua summoned the Gibeonites and said, *"Why did you deceive us by saying, 'We live a long way from you,' when actually you live near us? You are now under a curse: You will never cease to serve as woodcutters and water carriers for the house of my God."* (Joshua 9:22–23) The fruit of this deception would later have devastating effect upon the Gibeonites under the rule of Saul who tied to annihilate them. Saul's violation of the treaty was an issue that had consequences for the entire nation. Later King David needed to respond to the situation (2 Samuel 21:1–3) in order to remove the famine and bring healing to the land (2 Samuel 21:1, 14). Sin that is not properly addressed can have generational consequences! This is a huge spiritual principle that cannot be ignored.

How important it is that we cry out as the Psalmist did in Psalm 141:9—*"Keep me from the snares they have laid for me, from the traps set by evildoers."* In this day and age the people of God are regularly being trapped as they lean on their own understanding and do not ask God the right questions (Proverbs 3:5–6), or, as Jeremiah 10:21 puts it—*"The shepherds are senseless and do not inquire of the Lord; so they do not prosper and all their flock is scattered."* As a result, confusion has the right to rule and reign because a demon was knocking at the door and no one recognized its clothing and did not see through the deception of its food offering!

> When we are under deception, we are under the act of deceiving and also in the state of being deceived.

JUST WHAT EXACTLY IS DECEPTION?

The word deception is based on the verb *deceive.* When used with an object, it means "to deliberately cause (someone) to believe something that is not true, especially for personal gain." (Oxford Dictionary[2]) It is an act or intention to give somebody else a mistaken impression concerning something that appears to be true but in fact is not true.

The origin of this word comes from Middle English and based on the Old French word *deceivre* which is from the Latin *decipere* which means "to catch, ensnare, cheat."[3] Therefore, the whole intention of deception is to make somebody believe something that is not true, or to make somebody have a wrong idea about somebody else or about something else. (Oxford Advanced Learners Dictionary[4]) When we are under deception, we are under the act of deceiving and also in the state of being deceived. This is a fraud for the authentic, something based on partial truth. This is why most people do not readily see when deception is taking place.

SCRIPTURE SAYS DECEPTION IS REAL

The Bible provides numerous warnings to the people of God concerning deception. In Genesis 29:25 there is this fascinating discussion between Jacob and Laban concerning Laban's daughter Leah. Jacob had fully expected Rachel to be given to him as his wife. *"What is this you have done to me? I served you for Rachel, didn't I? Why have you deceived me?"*

> In Genesis 31:20 we are told—*"...Jacob deceived Laban... by not telling him he was running away."*
>
> Genesis 31:26. *"Then Laban said to Jacob, 'What have you done? You've deceived me and you've carried off my daughters like captives in war. '"*
>
> In Leviticus 19:11 we are warned—*"Do not steal. Do not lie. Do not deceive one another."* Here we find that the laws for social living, either at an individual or a corporate level, include the mandate not to deceive other people.
>
> Numbers 25 gives us the account of the people of Israel being seduced by the Moabites into worshipping the Baal of Peor and indulging in sexual immorality with the Moabite women. God indicates in verse 18 that His people were deceived by the Midianites. So often this is the case with the people of Israel throughout the Old Testament when they are seduced and deceived by other people, being influenced or even assimilating their lifestyle and forms of worship.

In 1 Samuel 28 we have the account of Saul and the witch of Endor who cries out, *"Why have you deceived me? You are Saul!"* (v12) Saul had disguised himself (v8) in order for her to consult a spirit.

Psalm 49:5–6 states: *"Why should I fear when evil days come, when wicked deceivers surround me—those who trust in their wealth and boast of their great riches?"* Here we see that the issue of deception can also involve the issue of wealth and pride.

Proverbs 14:5 clarifies that truth and deception are opposites—*"A truthful witness does not deceive, but a false witness pours out lies."*

Proverbs 26:18–19 indicate the seriousness in the eyes of God concerning deception—*"Like a madman shooting firebrands or deadly arrows is a man who deceives his neighbor and says, 'I was only joking!'"* In other words, deception is not a joking matter in the eyes of God.

Isaiah 19:13–14. Here we see that God holds Egypt responsible for her leaders who deceive those under them. The fruit of deception is serious— *"The officials of Zoan have become fools, the leaders of Memphis are deceived; the cornerstones of her peoples have led Egypt astray. The Lord has poured into them a spirit of dizziness..."*

In Jeremiah 9:4–6 there is a serious wake–up call concerning the issue of *deception* even amongst those who would seem to be friends. *"Beware of your friends; do not trust your brothers. For every brother is a deceiver and every friend a slanderer. Friend deceives friend, and no one speaks the truth. They have taught their tongues to lie; they weary themselves with sinning. You live in the midst of deception; in their deceit they refuse to acknowledge me, declares the Lord."*

Jeremiah 29:8–9 is a warning from the Lord since it involves the prophets—*"...do not let the prophets and diviners among you deceive you. Do not listen to the dreams you encourage them to have. They are prophesying lies to you in my name. I have not sent them, declares the Lord."*

> Jeremiah 37:9 has God addressing fantasy thinking in these words, *"This is what the Lord says: 'Do not deceive yourselves thinking; The Babylonians will surely leave us.' They will not!"* So often, people tend to deceive themselves into believing something that is fundamentally not true. Inevitably, we suffer the consequences.
>
> Jeremiah 49:16. *"The terror you inspire and the pride of your heart have deceived you...Though you build your nest as high as the eagle's, from there I will bring you down, declares the Lord."* Here we see that pride and deception go hand in hand but, in the end, they will not escape God's correction.
>
> Obadiah 1:7. *"All your allies will force you to the border; your friends will deceive and overpower you; those who eat your bread will set a trap for you, but you will not detect it."* It is very interesting to note that the prophecy of Obadiah is centered upon an ancient feud between Edom and Israel. Here we recall that the Edomites were descendants of Esau who carried a grudge against Israel due to the manner in which Jacob had cheated their ancestor Esau of his birthright. Again, this is a prime example of an on–going generational consequence that is the result of deception.

So far we have reviewed just a few verses from the Old Testament that highlight the issue of deception in the eyes of the Lord. Whether it is connected with pride, arrogance, lies, money, sex, relationships with people who worship foreign gods or just a result of being wooed by one's own fantasy thinking, deception which is based upon partial truth finds its origin in Genesis 3:13, *"Then the Lord God said to the woman, 'What is this you have done?' The woman said, 'The serpent deceived me, and I ate.'"* The issue of deception, therefore, was released throughout humanity due to the fall of man from the grace and presence of God who is all Truth.

Jesus continues this warning in the New Testament, which then is reinforced throughout the Epistles and the Book of Revelation.

Matthew 24:4–5. *"Jesus answered: 'Watch out that no–one deceives you. For many will come in my name, claiming, 'I am the Christ,' and will deceive many."*

Matthew 24:11. *"And many false prophets will appear and deceive many people."* In the end times, Jesus clearly is indicating that deception will be on the increase, even within the church.

Matthew 24:24. As we have already seen, this is a very searching word from Jesus himself. *"For false Christs and false prophets will appear and perform great signs and miracles to deceive even the elect—if that were possible."*

Romans 7:11. *"For sin, seizing the opportunity afforded by the commandment, deceived me, and through the commandment put me to death."* Here in Romans 7, Paul is giving his profound teaching concerning the issue of struggling with sin. In this verse he is making it quite clear that sin and deceptions go together and that this can only lead to death.

Romans 16:18. In the context of this passage, Paul is referring to those who cause divisions within the church and who can contradict the teaching that is fundamental to the Christian faith. *"For such people are not serving our Lord Christ, but their own appetites. By smooth talk and flattery they deceive the minds of naïve people."*

1 Corinthians 3:18. In a similar vein Paul is warning people not to indulge in self–deception—*"Do not deceive yourselves. If any one of you thinks he is wise by the standards of age, he should become a "fool" so that he may become wise."*

1 Corinthians 6:9–10. This is a particularly challenging verse in this day and age of relativism and compromise within the church. *"Do you not know that the wicked will not inherit the kingdom of God? Do not be deceived: Neither the sexually immoral nor idolaters nor adulterers nor male prostitutes nor homosexual offenders nor thieves nor the greedy nor drunkards nor slanderers nor swindlers will inherit the kingdom of God."* This verse makes it very hard to ignore the mandate of Scripture concerning sexuality from God's

point of view. Anything less than this point of view is based upon deception!

Galatians 6:3. This verse challenges every person at the core of their humanity. *"If anyone thinks he is something when he is nothing, he deceives himself."*

Galatians 6:7. Paul continues in this line of thinking by saying, *"Do not be deceived: God cannot be mocked. A man reaps what he sows."*

A lifestyle lived outside the parameters of godly living is not a lifestyle that the people of God can partner with at any level of life.

Ephesians 5:6. *"Let no one deceive you with empty words, for because of such things God's wrath comes on those who are disobedient."* In verses 3– 7 of this chapter, Paul is making it very clear about our position in Christ and our position with each other. In the end he says clearly in verse 7, *"Therefore do not be partners with them."* In other words, a lifestyle lived outside the parameters of godly living is not a lifestyle that the people of God can partner with at any level of life. A sobering reminder!

Colossians 2:4. *"I tell you this so that no one may deceive you by fine–sounding arguments."* In this first part of Colossians chapter 2, Paul is saying quite categorically that any argument that removes our thinking from the centrality of Christ, is an argument based upon deception.

2 Thessalonians 2:3. *"Don't let anyone deceive you in any way, for that day will not come, until the rebellion occurs and the man of lawlessness is revealed, the man doomed to destruction."* In the context of 2 Thessalonians 2: 1–12, we find that the whole subject of deception and lawlessness and counterfeit miracles, signs and wonders (v9), requires God's response in sending a powerful delusion so that people will believe the lie (v11). When people

choose to delight in wickedness, they will reap the harvest of that belief. (v12)

2 Timothy 3:13. *"While evil men and imposters will go from bad to worse, deceiving and being deceived."* This verse is in the context of godlessness and deception in the last days that will be on the increase as the return of Christ nears.

1 John 1:8. *"If we claim to be without sin, we deceive ourselves and the truth is not in us."* As we have already seen in Romans 3:23 we have all sinned and come short of the glory of God. Any belief system that is contrary to what God has said is based upon deception. Consequently, man then becomes the potter and God is the clay.

Revelation 13:14. *"Because of the signs he was given power to do on behalf of the first beast, he deceived the inhabitants of the earth..."* Deception will continue and increase in these end days affecting everyone.

Revelation 20:8. Even prior to his eternal punishment, Satan himself will at the end of the millennium *"...go out to deceive the nations in the four corners of the earth..."*

When the parameters and boundaries God has determined for His people are forgotten, trespassed, compromised or simply ignored, then the subsequent consequences affect the individual, the family, the church, the business, the city, and even the nation.

DECEPTION IS A COMMON PRACTICE

Fishing and hunting both involve deception. A fish may think it is about to catch a tasty meal when in fact it is being lured into a death trap! Once the bait is in the mouth of the fish, it is caught—hook, line and sinker. People, who go hunting for ducks, geese and other forms of wildlife, often use camouflage clothing and decoys in order to hide their presence. Duck and geese hunters use a certain type of noise maker that will lure the unsuspecting feathered creatures in their direction. They will even use false ducks and geese and place them on the water. If a bird gets too close, shots will be fired, and its goose is quickly cooked!

Even in nature, all varieties of deception can be detected. On one occasion during a visit to the Daintree Rainforest in Australia, I was fascinated to learn about a spider which creates a type of web that looks like bird droppings so that birds will not see the spider as a potential meal. However, the same deception lures ants and flies into thinking they are coming for a meal—when in fact they become the meal! The web is a deterrent to one—but a lure to the other. It survives through deception!

Occasionally I watch a reality television program in which storage lockers are put up for auction when the rent has no longer been paid. At times, there are quite amazing finds in these lockers. However, what amuses and amazes me is that so many of the people placing bids are out to deceive one another—even by their own admission. They move, gesticulate, wink their eyes, shift their hands and even try to say things just loud enough to be heard by others... in order to fool other bidders.

Deception is a way of life in much of society today. So much of life as we know it seems to be subject to branding by this intruder. As we have seen in this chapter, this has been a major trap for the people of God over many millennia. History seems to affirm that famous line in the epic poem *Marmion, A Tale of Flodden Field*[5], by Sir Walter Scott published in 1808 and which was based upon a great disaster in Scottish history—"Oh, what a tangled web we weave, When first we practice to deceive."

BUT WHY ARE THE "ELECT" DECEIVED?

We need to learn why deception can catch the people of God off guard, especially as we near the return of Jesus Christ. We need to look at this in more depth in order to learn how to address it appropriately. We also need to ensure that the parameters of God's life and work in us and through us will not become subject to counterfeit by the enemy

---

1. *The New English Bible*, New York, Oxford University Press, 1971

2. *Oxford Dictionaries British and World English* as found on Google search engine – http://www.oxforddictionaries.com
3. Ibid.
4. Ibid.
5. *Marmion, A Tale of Flodden Field* Author: Sir Walter Scott – published in 1808 (Source – Wikipedia) www.in.wikipedia.org

3

THE TOXICITY OF DECEPTION *and its Antidote*

WHO IS SATAN?

A brief trip through Scripture would highlight references to Satan as the Adversary, the Lawless One, the evil one (1 John 5:19), and even the Ruler of the kingdom of the air. (Ephesians 2:2) According to 1 Chronicles 21:1, he incites the people of God; he roams throughout the earth (Job 1:7), and he seeks to condemn those who are blameless, upright, those who fear God and shun evil, and those of integrity. (Job 1:8; Job 2:3) Apparently, he can present himself before the Lord (Job 2:1), he can rise up against nations and incite the people of God to do what is contrary to God's purpose for them (1 Chronicles 21:1), he can inflict physical issues upon us (Job 2:7), he will accuse us (Zechariah 3:1) and will do all this relentlessly—even day and night (Revelation 12:10); he is also a stumbling block to what God wants to do in and through our lives. (Matthew 16:23)

Matthew 4:3 specifically refers to the devil as the tempter. In Matthew 4:1–11, Mark 1:12–13 and Luke 4:1–13, we find Satan tempting Jesus as the Son of God to capitulate to a counterfeit plan in the areas of

His Messiahship...as an economic Messiah, as a wonder–working Messiah, and as a political Messiah. In so doing, Satan attempted to shift homage to himself and away from God's eternal plan of salvation for humanity.

Since Satan has access to the world (the cosmos—meaning structures and systems of life), he is relentless in his activity in our midst.

Satan can bind up people from entering their destiny (Luke 13:16) and he can enter our lives when we least expect it. (Luke 22:3; Acts 5:3)

He will attempt to blind people from the knowledge of the glory of the living God (Acts 26:4–18; 2 Corinthians 4:4) and he even masquerades as an angel of light. (2 Corinthians 11:14)

He will attempt to block God's plan for our life (1 Thessalonians 2:18) and, according to Paul in 2 Thessalonians 2:9–10, *"The coming of the lawless one will be in accordance with the work of Satan displayed in all kinds of counterfeit miracles, signs and wonders, and in every sort of evil that deceives those that are perishing..."*

However, Isaiah 54:16 reminds us that God is still in charge, and can even use the devil to His advantage. Having an Adversary can be a means of our experiencing the Grace of God at work in us. (2 Corinthians 12:7–9)

Since Satan has access to the world (the *cosmos*—meaning structures and systems of life), he is relentless in his activity in our midst. He constantly prowls around like a roaring lion looking for someone to devour (1 Peter 5:8). Therefore, he has the right of access on the physical realm (land, cities, and nations) to the degree that we give access to him through our sin and fallen stewardship. He is not God's equal but he is powerful. Through the Scriptures we have examined, we now have a clue behind the issue of deception that has become so rampant in the church today.

NOT ALL THAT IS SUPERNATURAL IS OF GOD!

In Exodus chapters 7 to 11, we see the battle between Moses and the Pharaoh and his appointed magicians. A myriad of supernatural events take place. The magicians were able to counterfeit almost every miraculous deed of the Lord until it came to the Passover. This is a sober wake–up call for the church. Simply because something is supernatural does not necessarily mean it comes from God!

Leviticus 10:1 gives us a graphic insight into the misuse of the supernatural… *"Aaron's sons Nadab and Abihu took their censors, put fire in them and added incense; and they offered unauthorized fire before the Lord, contrary to his command."* As we follow through that brief passage, we find that they undertook a spiritual practice in an unlawful and unholy manner. They were dealing with the supernatural but not in a way that brought honour and glory to God. When it comes to an understanding of the depth of our relationship with a holy God, we cannot avoid these words of caution from God given through Moses to His people. Verses 10–11 make this clear: *"You must distinguish between the holy and the common, between the unclean and the clean, and you must teach the Israelites all the decrees the Lord has given them through Moses."* As far as the sons of Aaron were concerned, the fire that they handled was real but it was both unauthorized and unholy. A misunderstanding of this will deceive even the elect (Matthew 24:24), and once again simply because something is supernatural does not mean its DNA is of the living God.

We have seen that Satan is behind all kinds of counterfeit miracles, signs and wonders. Therefore, in 2 Thessalonians 2:9–11, Paul issues his sober warning that not all supernatural events are initiated by the Lord. Satan masquerades as an angel of light (2 Corinthians 11:14), or, putting it another way, he is a wolf in sheep's clothing and so tries to fit into our midst without being recognized.

A MANDATE TO TEST SPIRITS

Little wonder, therefore, that John wrote these words of warning—*"Dear friends, do not believe every spirit, but test the spirits to see whether they are from God, because many false prophets have gone out into the world. This is how you can recognize the Spirit of God: Every spirit that acknowledges that Jesus Christ has come in the flesh is from God, but every spirit that does not acknowledge Jesus is not from God. This is the spirit of the antichrist, which you have heard is coming and even now is already in the world."* (1 John 4:1–3) Part of the work of the Holy Spirit that works in and through us as described in 1 Corinthians 12, is enabling us to distinguish between spirits. (1 Corinthians 12:10) Throughout Scripture God has always given us this warning, particularly when acknowledging the existence of spiritual offices and spiritual gifts that tend to operate in the supernatural such as the prophetic. Ponder these sober warnings from the Lord himself:

> Isaiah 8:19— *"When men tell you to consult mediums and spiritists, who whisper and mutter, should not a people inquire of their God? Why consult the dead on behalf of the living?"* Why, indeed, did Saul consult the witch of Endor (1 Samuel 28)?
>
> Deuteronomy 13:1–3— *"If a prophet, or one who foretells by dreams, appears among you and announces to you a miraculous sign or wonder, and if the sign or wonder of which he has spoken takes place, and he says, 'Let us follow other gods' (gods you have not known) 'and let us worship them,' you must not listen to the words of that prophet or dreamer. The Lord your God is testing you to find out whether you love him with all your heart and with all your soul."*
>
> Jeremiah 14:14— *"Then the Lord said to me, 'The prophets are prophesying lies in my name. I have not sent them or appointed them or spoken to them. They are prophesying to you false visions, divinations, idolatries and the delusions of their own minds...'"* God has an obvious displeasure at those who prophesy words in His name that never came from Him in the first place.

In the context of Jeremiah 23:9–40, God gives harsh words when it comes to those who prophesy in an ungodly manner or with an unholy power. Ponder these searching words in verse 10: *"The land is full of adulterers, because of the curse the land lies parched and the pastures in the desert are withered. The prophets follow an evil course and use their power unjustly. Both prophet and priest are godless..."* He goes on to say in verse 15 that it is due to the prophets of Jerusalem that ungodliness spread across the land. (v15) He says in verse 16, *"Do not listen to what the prophets are prophesying to you; they fill you with false hopes. They speak visions from their own minds, not from the mouth of the Lord. They keep saying to those who despise me, 'The Lord says: You will have peace.' And to all who follow the stubbornness of their hearts they say, 'No harm will come to you.'"* The whole of Jeremiah 23 needs to be carefully considered due to the seriousness of utilizing the prophetic in an ungodly and unholy manner.

Consider all of Ezekiel Chapter 13. Verses 3 and 4 are quite clear: *"This is what the Sovereign Lord says, 'Woe to the foolish prophets who follow their own spirit and have seen nothing! Your prophets, O Israel, are like jackals among ruins.'"* God's view on this is even more clear in verses 8 and 9: *"Therefore this is what the Sovereign Lord says: 'Because of your false words and lying visions, I am against you, declares the Sovereign Lord. My hand will be against the prophets who see false visions and utter lying divinations. They will not belong to the council of my people or be listed in the records of the house of Israel...'"*

A glance at any reasonable Concordance will provide many examples of false prophecy referred to in Scripture. However, one of the most challenging and serious passages concerning the use of the supernatural in an unholy and unwarranted manner is found in Matthew 7:23—*"Then I will tell them plainly, 'I never knew you. Away from me, you evildoers!' "*

To understand this Scripture, we need to look at it in the context of verses 21 to 23.

> *"Not everyone who says to me, 'Lord, Lord,' will enter the kingdom of heaven, but only he who does the will of my Father who is in heaven. Many will say to me on that day, 'Lord, Lord, did we not prophesy in your name, and in your name drive out demons and perform many miracles?' Then I will tell them plainly, 'I never knew you. Away from me, you evildoers!'"*

There is an issue here of authority and intimacy. They are intended to go hand in hand. It is not just a matter of referring to Jesus as "Lord" but actually implementing His will here on earth. According to verse 22 many will call Him "Lord" and justify themselves by saying they prophesied in the name of Jesus, drove out demons in His name and performed many miracles. And yet in verse 23 Jesus says that these people are evildoers and He never knew them. The Complete Jewish Bible[1] translates verse 23 in this way—*"Then I will tell them to their faces, I never knew you! Get away from Me, you workers of lawlessness!"* Similarly, The New American Standard[2] translation says, *"And then I will declare to them, I never knew you; depart from me, you who practice lawlessness."* However, the New Living Translation[3] says *"But I will reply, I never knew you. Go away; the things you did were unauthorized."*

Lawlessness is a complete ignoring of the Law and Covenant as set down in relationship between God and His people.

A variety of words such as wickedness, lawlessness, iniquity, evil doers and law breakers (Holman Christian Standard version[4]) indicate that the actions of these people ministering in the name of Jesus have met with His anger and wrath. The use of the word "know" (from the Greek *ginosko*) can mean in English *to know, to allow, to be aware of, to be sure of*, as well as to *have knowledge of*. Reference 1097 in Strong's Greek Lexicon[5] refers to *ginosko* as "a prolonged form of a primary verb, to 'know' (absolutely) in a great variety of applications and with many implications (as follow, with others not thus clearly expressed): *allow, be aware (of), feel (have) know(–ledge), perceived, be resolved, can speak, be sure, understand.*"

Clearly, this issue of Jesus not acknowledging or knowing these people is based on the fact they are working within lawlessness. Lawlessness according to Strong's Greek Lexicon[6] (459 and 460) means *working not subject to the (Jewish) law, being a transgressor* and *being wicked*, therefore *working lawlessly*. In other words, there is a complete ignoring of the Law and Covenant as set down in relationship between God and His people. Therefore, these people are utilizing what is potentially an "empowering" from the spirit realm, but not as authorized by God Himself. From God's perspective, this is highly serious!

Putting it plainly, Matthew 7:21–23 can refer to miracles, great things, mighty works, wonderful works, salvation, healing, deliverance and prophesying. The context of this entire passage which is under the sub–heading of a tree and its fruit, begins in chapter 7 verse 15 with these words from Jesus: *"Watch out for false prophets. They come to you in sheep's clothing, but inwardly they are ferocious wolves. By their fruit you will recognize them... A good tree cannot bear bad fruit, and a bad tree cannot bear good fruit... Thus, by their fruit you will recognize them."* (Matthew 7:15–20)

In light of all this, therefore, we need to ask an important question. With the end times now shaping the day and age in which we live, have we ventured into a time in which—wittingly or unwittingly—many have begun to engage in the use of extra biblical theology, or experiential theology?

RECOGNIZING EXTRA BIBLICAL AND EXPERIENTIAL THEOLOGY

If we take a simple definition of "theology" as being the truth about God—as revealed in Scripture—then we establish a plumb line that reveals God's character—His word—His activity etc. (Amos 7:7–8) The term "extra biblical", implies utilizing a proof text for the works of God, which lie beyond the parameters of Scripture as revealed in the Old and New testaments.

Problems begin when the extra biblical becomes subjectively "experiential" and then subtly goes on to become increasingly "doctrinal".

Granted, however, there are many practices and aspects of the 21st century church which are not found in Scripture word for word, but which have become part of our contextualized church culture over these last several centuries. For example, the term "Sunday School" is not found in Scripture, but educating children in the knowledge and ways of the Lord certainly is found in Scripture. Robert Raikes introduced the idea of Sunday School well over a hundred years ago.[7] Scripture does not give the "mechanics" on how to conduct a church service, a subject upon which different denominations have developed their own opinions! Similarly, as long as we baptize or celebrate the Last Supper practising the essential sacraments in our own traditions, and are found to be people of prayer, praise, and worship, and who meet together regularly, then the manner in which we do all this may be "extra biblical", however none of it is contrary to Scripture.

Therefore we are determining the difference between something being "anti–biblical" as opposed to it being extra biblical. However, the problems begin when the extra biblical becomes subjectively "experiential" and then subtly goes on to become increasingly "doctrinal". The problem is that if we stray beyond what God Himself has said then our subjective experience creates new parameters of acceptable practice—over and above that of Scripture. Gnosticism and Postmodernism have been guilty of this for generations. In other words, I believe something to be true simply because I have "experienced" it—or at least simply because I *think / believe* I have experienced it.

But, does that mean it is true in the sense of the biblical plumb line, or is this simply relativism and subjectivity, and a matter of "feeling good"?

POSITIVE EXPERIENTIAL THEOLOGY

The Biblical Mandate to preach, teach, heal, deliver, pray

Therefore, can "Experiential Theology" be positive without straying from the safeguards of the Bible? Yes, if it is defined within an understanding of theology that is experienced through the practical application of the truth that is ***IN*** God's Word...**but not over and beyond** God's revealed Word. In other words, it is *NOT* to be a theology simply based upon observation and experience, independent of the Word of God.

For instance, for those in healing and deliverance, clear instruction comes from the Word of God (Scripture) that both these areas of ministry are essential components of the kingdom of God, and, it is biblically correct to cast out demons and to heal the sick. When we undertake the application of this, then understandably our "experience" or practise may differ from one ministry to another. This actually can even serve to ***deepen our understanding*** of the bare instruction Jesus gave to His disciples to go and heal the sick, which in due course became the mandate of the entire body of Christ.

NEGATIVE EXPERIENTIAL THEOLOGY

Experiential theology in the negative sense is theology deduced from observation or practice which strays beyond what the faith and praxis of the history of our faith as once revealed, actually accepts as being "orthodox". A leader once said to me that for him experience came first and after that he would fit in the doctrine. While that sounds acceptable and inviting, what and

> An over–emphasis of "grace" without responsibility... ushers in a modern version of antinomianism.

where are the safeguards? His statement increasingly troubled me since it was subtly suggesting that what is contained in the Bible is not sufficient and we can do anything we choose—or experience—and justify what we do. The danger of this is that it may lead to an over–emphasis of "grace" without responsibility, which ushers in a modern version of antinomianism.

This subtle shift is of great concern, since it moves people towards what can be termed as "**Postmodernism Gnosticism**", in which humanism and personal subjectivity reign without any real parameters or accepted limitations; a developing trend of the 21st Century! In other words, if I "feel it" or "sense it" or "experience it"—then it must be real! This has led some practitioners in the church to say, "We look for the sign or miracle first—then afterwards fit the theology into our equation!" This, as history has shown, can be a dangerous way of thinking! It could also well be what Jesus was warning against in Matthew 7:21–23. Furthermore, it is very possibly what will end up deceiving the elect! (Matthew 24:24)

Subjectivity becomes a real issue when we stray from the plumb line... from the history of our faith once received...from the canons...from the sixty–six books of the Bible...from the ancient formularies that were the mainstay of the developing church over many generations—the Nicene Creed, Athanasian Creed, Apostles' Creed etc. All this ensured heresy was kept out and orthodoxy was retained—no matter how enticing or attractive the desire to "bend the rules" may have been.

When one rests on subjectivity with a hint of biblical integrity thrown in to make things "appear" acceptable—at what point do we then determine what is biblically correct or experientially relative, and therefore acceptable? Again, just because it "works" does not necessarily mean it is of God. We stray dangerously towards a type of potential leadership infrastructure which continues to define itself more by experiential practices than by biblical boundaries.

WHY WE NEED TO BE CONCERNED

The concern over experiential theology arises when someone has an experience that is attributed to the working of the Holy Spirit ("This is what the Holy Spirit has shown me—has led me to do"...etc) then this experience or expression of spiritual activity may become for them normative, then genuine and then unquestionable.

When it reaches the last stage—that of being unquestionable—it is not difficult to choose any random portion of Scripture and make it "fit" with the experience. This invariably overrides the wider context of Scripture—and the testing of that portion from other passages elsewhere in the Bible. With this practice, the individual uses Scripture independently, in isolation to what others may say, and in isolation to what the history of the faith may indicate.

In Scripture, we have been given a standard by which we are to judge and discern both our own and others' experiences.

Rather than screening the experience through Scripture and generally accepted interpretations, it becomes a doctrine. Subsequently an experiential form of theology has taken on a dogmatic aspect. Thus it creates a new praxis acceptable for this day and age, even if it is not in keeping with that of earlier generations.

WHAT, THEN, SHOULD BE OUR STANDARD?

In Scripture, we have been given a standard by which we are to judge and discern both our own and others' experiences. In other words, each experience should be tested against Scripture and discarded if it does not have any solid foundation in the Word of God. In other words, we lean into the Lord for His understanding and seek corporate counsel as we unpack what Scripture means. In the case of negative experiential theology, the experience forms the doctrine and therefore the theology. It is based on the belief that God is continually expanding on and giving new revelation that goes beyond the written Word. The assumption is made that "if it works, then it has to be good and it has to be God at work through the power of the Holy Spirit." History shows this to be an ongoing cycle of tension.

CAUTION RE: SIGNS AND WONDERS

If we believe all signs and wonders are a continuing revelation of God at work in our midst, then we are very easily drawn to accept that, whatever is demonstrated or revealed through a sign or wonder or a prophetic word, must be doctrinally sound. Therefore there are no longer any boundaries—no absolutes. This results in confusion, along with an undefined authority in our lives. What authority do we follow? Is the authority in which we become established the "expression of experience" or is it in God's Word? A dangerous atmosphere is created where those not solidly grounded in Scripture become primarily seekers of signs and wonders. The Bible clearly warns us not to seek after signs and wonders, nonetheless when these follow the proclamation of the Word of God, they are indeed an indicator of the kingdom of God at work in our midst. On the other hand, deception occurs when the basis of faith is based purely upon signs and wonders without reference to the One to whom the signs and wonders should point, and at times in the absence of genuine repentance.

Experience should come out of our biblical foundation. By embracing experiential theology, we are causing a generation to become disconnected from foundational truth. That gap will continue to widen since, in the years that follow, it will become increasingly difficult for this generation to instruct and impart truth to those that follow. Revelation 22:18–19 clearly tells of the severe penalty of either adding to or taking away from the Word of God.

A LIST OF DANGERS

In light of what has been discussed so far, here are some areas of deception that are challenging the Church in the 21st century:

> The Victorious view of eschatology embraces the belief that the church will rise in victory, power and maturity before the return of Christ.

Beware of the term *Post Scriptural era*. Simply put, this means that the Bible in itself is not sufficient for determining what is and what is not of God.

Using the term *Extra–Biblical Theology* to justify supernatural experiences can quickly change the interpretation of Scripture. For example, this lies behind the practice of both commanding and worshipping angels in private and corporate settings. Scripture is clear that angels are not to be worshipped. They are real, and there is a significant interaction of angels with humanity throughout Scripture. However, never at any time do we command them—that is the prerogative of God alone.

The first two chapters of Paul's letter to the Colossians combat the false teachings of the Gnostics who were threatening to lead the Colossians away from the truth concerning the sufficiency of Christ for salvation. Paul was addressing the dangers of dualism—the separation of matter and spirit—as well as challenging the Gnostic doctrine which encouraged people to worship angels. (Colossians 2:18) If we build prophecy simply upon experience and "secret knowledge" then we have removed all the safeguards and boundaries for determining what is of God, and what is not of God.

We must ensure that we have not allowed the Word of God to become a word from "a god". The subtlety is to start humanizing Scripture to our level and thus humanizing God to our level. The fear of the Lord is then removed from our understanding of the Word of God, ending up with no biblical plumb line of reference. (Amos 7:7–8) In other words, experiential theology not firmly based in the Word of God means that we can become like God and bring Him down to our level. We are therefore self–deified as the potter, with God rendered as the clay.

All this can lead to a deception in our eschatology. The Victorious view of eschatology embraces the belief that the church will rise in victory, power and maturity before the return of Christ. This implies that every nation will come to Christ before His return, a belief also known as post–millennialism. It requires us to believe that it is up to the church to determine through our actions when the Lord shall return. Although God is fully sovereign, through this form of "open theism", God deliberately restricts His actions until we tell Him what to do. This can lead to a form of triumphalism and eventually to the subtle thinking that we are exempt from persecution.

This is based on the belief that, after the fall of Jerusalem in AD 70, much of Matthew 24–25 and Revelation 4–18 were all fulfilled. Consequently we now live beyond that time of history. In turn, a form of high level Dominion thinking follows, suggesting that since Satan was defeated by the cross, his power on earth is now dwindling. Thus, through the declaration of the testimony of the church, we are able to overcome every work of Satan and bring cities and nations into their destiny in Christ. It is then that Christ will return. However, Daniel 12:10 disproves Dominion theology and victorious eschatology in that, *"Many will be purified, made spotless and refined, but the wicked will continue to be wicked. None of the wicked will understand but those who are wise will understand."*

The problem is that there *is* truth in what we have just said. However, it is partial truth mixed with suggestive subjectivity.

In early 2012, I circulated a survey to leaders in different nations asking them to list what they felt were the top issues facing the Church in the 21st century. Here are the conclusions from the responses that we received from several of those leaders.

1. Scriptural/biblical integrity—2 Timothy 3:1–7—having a form of Godliness but denying the power thereof—having no knowledge of the truth. No plumb line integrity, allowing for the entrance of deception.

2. The lack of preaching the Word of God while being seduced by unorthodox doctrines of God. Therefore a need for proper apologetics—defending the truth based upon the faith once received. Ultimately this would challenge such relevant topics as marriage, abortion, euthanasia, all of which challenge the relevance of Scripture.

3. A "non–conversion" issue developing within evangelical Christianity, highlighting some of the concerns coming from the seeker–sensitive approach. In some cases "incomplete" conversions have resulted, with no real deliverance from the old life to the new life, resulting in a diluted form of discipleship.

4. Doctrinal perplexities such as a lack of teaching concerning the cross and the resurrection, thus opening the door to the extra–biblical and experiential theology. This raises questions such as: *Is Jesus Christ really the Way, the Truth and the Life? Is he really God? Is belief in Jesus essential for eternal life?*

5. Secularism has become the "new gospel". We seem to live in an increasingly confused, complacent, convenient and compromised Christian culture. If the church ceases becoming an authentic prophetic catalyst in society, then sin is accommodated at all levels of life. What about Isaiah 5:20? *"Woe to those who call evil good and good evil, who put darkness for light and light for darkness, who put bitter for sweet and sweet for bitter."*

6. An unbalanced teaching gives rise to a lack of discernment—the need for the gift of the discernment of spirits. Without this, false teachers, false leaders, false prophecies, false experiences and false visions will all continue to increase and gain momentum within the church and subsequent issues such as the worship of angels will then increase.

7. Knowing the difference between the fear of the Lord and the fear of man and having the courage to confront issues defined by God as sin.

8. The issue of the church and its attitude towards Israel which can be termed as God's thermometer and barometer in society today.
9. A lack of proper accountability within leadership circles in order to avoid the abuse of new versions of the shepherding movement.
10. The rising concern of lawlessness and entitlement which results in a lack of a true understanding of discipleship and dying to self. As a result a more "experientially–based" Christianity emerges with the lack of biblically–based mentoring.
11. The millions of "church dropouts" who are becoming increasingly discouraged with the status and integrity of the four walled church.
12. The global and biblical implications concerning the current economy, politics, world religions, and the emerging spiritual deception behind Islam.
13. Turning away from a soulish declarative ministry that lacks a passionate prayer life at both personal and corporate level. Prayer based on intimacy is one that inquires after the Lord rather than working on presumption and pride in the place of God.
14. The need of a proper theology of death in light of the growing popular belief that we can, at random, raise the dead and offer them a second chance of salvation. The question is whether a new form of purgatory, indulgences and universalism has entered into the church.
15. Entering the third heaven on a human–initiated basis and accessing the counsel of the saints at random such as St. Paul, St. Matthew, Abraham and Samson, and other Saints of the past. This opens up the subject of necromancy and familiar spirits.
16. The issue of transferrable anointings and visiting graveyards of people such as Evan Roberts and William Branham in order to resurrect a past anointing.

These are all examples of key areas within the Church today in which deception will try and gain a foothold. Let's not forget that it is the father of lies who rules the world at this time (John 8:44), and he will try and deceive us with counterfeits of the real Bread of Life! We have now seen some of the consequences that can arise as a result, especially in a season during which people are hungry for signs and wonders. The problem is that when we wittingly or unwittingly embrace a counterfeit, we give the enemy spiritual authority which leads to the counterfeit of the true healing and freedom and transformation God has planned for our lives. Just as we have learned from the banking industry whose employees are trained to recognize counterfeit money through handling and recognizing large quantities of the genuine, so, too, we must submit to the Good Shepherd, the Bread of Life, and immerse ourselves in His Word and Spirit. Then we will more readily identify the works of the enemy, and whatever is false will be quickly recognized. If we have followed a counterfeit it is important to confess this, and receive the Lord's forgiveness and release from all that is false and harmful to us and which will try and condemn us. In chapter 2, reference was made to deception being part of fishing and hunting! The fish may not receive a second chance, but through the Grace of God—we do!

"KIRK AND SPOCK KLINGON THEOLOGY"

Many of us have grown up with the television and movie series *Star Trek*. In keeping with Star Trek history, a race known as the Romulans developed a technology known as "cloaking" which subsequently was made available to the Klingons who then became identified as the race utilizing this cloaking device which allowed a space ship to remain hidden from its enemy. In other words, it was there but could not be seen! Enthusiasts of this series are familiar with the type of conversation between Captain Kirk and Mr. Spock (of the Federation Starship *Enterprise*) about a possible distortion seen on the screen which could be a Klingon vessel utilizing its cloaking device to render it effectively invisible. Kirk and Spock are not sure if something really is there. Until the shields of the *Enterprise* are put in place, the ship is vulnerable and the crew can be caught unawares if the enemy launches its photon torpedoes. My term "Klingon Theology," refers to that which 'sees' distortion, but where the shield of faith and the gift of discernment of spirits are missing because deception was not recognized quickly enough.

Distortion is deception! "Klingon theology" develops when the Word of God no longer frames our reference of reality.[8]

WHAT IS THE ANTIDOTE FOR ALL THIS?

Isaiah 8:20 says, *"To the law and to the testimony! If they do not speak according to this word, they have no light of dawn."*

Similarly, Titus 1:9 indicates: *"He must hold firmly to the trustworthy message as it has been taught, so that he can encourage others by sound doctrine and refute those who oppose it."* Paul instructs Timothy in 1 Timothy 6:20–21, *"Timothy, guard what has been entrusted to your care. Turn away from godless chatter and the opposing ideas of what is falsely called knowledge, which some have professed and in so doing have wandered from the faith."*

Similarly Paul says in 2 Timothy 3:16–17, *"All scripture is God–breathed and is useful for teaching, rebuking, correcting, and training in righteousness, so that the man of God may be thoroughly equipped for every good work."*

Why is this important? According to Paul in Ephesians 4:14, *"Then we will no longer be infants, tossed back and forth by the waves, and blown here and there by every wind of teaching* (KJV— *"every wind of doctrine"*) *and by the cunning and craftiness of men in their deceitful scheming..."* These and many other such similar Scriptures testify to the fact that the Word of God is the antidote for all forms of deception.

2 Kings 4:38–41 could well be a description of life today. There was a famine in the land. Elisha instructed his servant to put on a large pot of stew for the company of the prophets. Unfortunately, one of the people gathered some deceptively harmless–looking herbs and they ended up in the stew. When the food was consumed, it began to poison the people. There was death in the pot! All the ingredients looked fine, but the contents of the pot—describing life—was full of poison. The sobering lesson here is not to be distracted and deceived. However Elisha had the solution.

"Elisha said, 'Get some flour.' He put it into the pot and said, 'Serve it to the people to eat.' And there was nothing harmful in the pot." (2 Kings

4:41) It is the same solution for us today. Pour in the meal—pour in the flour—pour in the meal of life! It is the Risen Bread of Life which, when deposited into the vessel of life, cancels out all deception through the power of the Cross! This is the boundary line between life and death.

---

1. *Complete Jewish Bible* Translator: David H. Stern, Jewish New Testament Publications, Inc., Clarksville, Maryland USA, 1998 ISBN 0 19 529751 2
2. *New American Standard Version*, The Lockman Foundation; 1995 Printing as used on Bible Gateway Website www.biblegateway.com
3. *Living Translation*, Tyndale House Publishers, Inc. Wheaton, Illinois, 1996 ISBN 0 8423 4050 5
4. *Holman Christian Standard Bible* (HCSB) 1999,2000,2002, 2003,2009 Holman Bible Publishers, Nashville, Tennessee (Source – http://www.biblegateway.com
5. *Strong's Greek Lexicon* – Ref. # 1097 – www.studybible.info/strongs/G1097
6. *Strong's Greek Lexicon* – Ref. # 459 & 460 – www.studybible.info/strongs/G459 www.studybible.info/strongs/G460
7. Robert Raikes; Google search – www.infed.org/walking/wa–raikes.html
8. Star Trek and Klingon information – available at www.wikipedia.org/wiki/Klingon

4

GOD'S VIEW ON *Boundaries*

GOLF ANYONE?

Golf is a game of strategy. The more you play it, the more proficient you become. Similar to many other sports, golf is played according to a set of rules within physical boundaries. When the ball is hit "out of bounds", certain penalties apply. There are certain rules of etiquette and conduct in order for the game to be played correctly. Most golf courses have challenges and impediments such as water hazards, sand bunkers and various degrees of thick grass in the rough. The better the player, the more likely these pitfalls will be avoided.

Golf requires rules in order for us to reach proficiency. However, this is true for every aspect of life—right from the individual through to the corporate life of a nation. God has given us boundaries, not to be legalistic, but in order to release His highest purpose in and through us. Life has its pitfalls and challenges, but learning to respect and acknowledge God's boundaries leads to the abundant life He yearns for us to experience.

ABUNDANT LIFE

In John 10:9–10 we read these words, *"I am the gate; whoever enters through me will be saved. He will come in and go out, and find pasture. The thief comes only to steal and kill and destroy; I have come that they may have life, and have it to the full."* The Complete Jewish Bible[1] translates the last part of verse 10 in these words, *"I have come so that they may have life, life in its fullest measure."* With reference to the same verses, the Amplified Bible[2] ends with these words—*"I came that they might have and enjoy life and have it in abundance (to the full, till it overflows)."* The New American Standard Bible[3] translates these same words as:*"I came that they might have life, and have it abundantly."*

The intent of Jesus is for us to enjoy life in the fullest possible way, but this can only be achieved and received according to the conditions set down by the Lord Himself. In the context of this passage in John 10, we are told that Jesus is a gate for the sheep (v8), that we have to enter through this gate (v9) in order to be saved, and that we will be going in and coming out in order to find pasture—our fulfillment, our destiny, our purpose, the reason for our being. Verse 10 also infers that there is a thief—a killjoy, an adversary—someone who plans to steal, kill and destroy. This enemy wants to remove this destiny, fulfillment and abundance from us. Jesus explains the message saying that He has come in order that, through Him, this fullness of life can be received and enjoyed. The question is, are there "rules" or "boundaries" that we need to agree to in order to experience life in the manner God has promised?

We have seen already that we are living in a time of increasing momentum and it is a matter of urgency that we learn to read the signs of the times correctly and acknowledge that God is shaking the systems of the world in order to get our attention. We have also seen we are living in a generation in which deception is knocking at the door on a continual basis. We have seen the subtle way in which deception enters and then becomes an impediment and challenge. We have seen that often deception will come as a wolf in sheep's clothing. We have seen already that even the elect can be deceived. We have seen that even Jesus says many will come with the appearance of ministering in His name and signs will follow them but, in the end, He will say He did not know these people or give them His authorization. These are sobering indicators that God wants to get our attention in order for us to live life His way at a time in which there are so many distractions attempting to take our eyes off Jesus who is the Gate.

Today, we need to address the question of whether the Word of God is a boundary marker or merely a moveable goalpost.

There can be no place for any form of "Klingon theology" otherwise, as we saw in the last chapter, there can be death in the pot of life! At all levels of life today, we need to address the question of whether the Word of God is a boundary marker or merely a moveable goalpost developed out of subjective relativism?

Putting it another way, are we the potter or the clay? If we are still the clay, then the Potter has the right of access to our lives at every single level. Throughout the centuries of the Old Testament, God continually taught His people the ways of life that would lead them into their promised land. Not only that, His teaching was designed to bring them into the fullness of their role as the people of God. In this process, God has always given His people freedom of choice. He does this, even though the 'benefits' of living life according to our own set of rules leads to deception and then eventual death.

THE CARPENTER'S MARKER

While I am not particularly good at any form of carpentry, thankfully there are other members in our family who are very handy with tools! My father was trained as a civil engineer and draftsman, and on many occasions I would watch him develop something made out of wood. First he would design the layout on paper and then use that blueprint to create the finished product. There was a distinct line which became his reference point for completing the project correctly.

In Genesis 1:26–27 we read these words, *"Then God said, 'Let us make man in our image, in our likeness...' So God created man in his own image, in the image of God he created him; male and female he created them."* This means that we were created with design and purpose in mind. Even 1 Corinthians 11:7 informs us that man is the image and glory of God (His design). Jesus who is the second member of the Godhead came to dwell in our midst in order to show us what God is like. *"He is the image of the invisible God, the firstborn over all creation."* (Colossians 1:15) Putting it another way, Jesus is God who has come to visit us in the flesh.

Amazingly, man will attempt to copy God's design and even create the "finished product", attempting to self–deify himself determining his own boundary lines. The words of Isaiah 44:13 are fascinating—*"The carpenter measures with a line and makes an outline with a marker; he roughs it out with chisels and marks it with compasses. He shapes it in the form of man, of man in all his glory that it may dwell in a shrine."* As we shall see this inevitably leads to a deluded heart unable to detect what is a lie. (c.f. Isaiah 44:20)

However, just as God is specific in the manner in which He has designed us, so also He applies this same principle to the land itself. Ezekiel 39:15–16 states, *"As they go through the land, and one of them sees a human bone, he will set up a marker beside it until the gravediggers have buried it in the valley of Hamon Gog... And so they will cleanse the land."* Here we see a specific activity (cleansing the land) that takes place in an area that has been *marked out* in advance.

BEATING THE BOUNDS

According to Wikipedia, beating the bounds is an ancient custom still observed in some English and Welsh parishes. The members in the church community would walk the boundaries of the parish, usually led by the parish priest and church officials, to share the knowledge of where those boundaries lay, and to pray for protection and blessing for the people and businesses who lived within the jurisdiction of these boundary lines. While the earliest origins of beating the bounds go back as far as the Anglo–Saxon days, the church began to adopt the practice of maintaining its pastoral responsibility within a physical jurisdiction and asking God's blessing upon the land that was under its spiritual care.[4]

In Joshua 1:3–4 the Lord gives some very specific instructions to Joshua—*"I will give you every place where you set your foot as I promised Moses. Your territory will extend from the desert to Lebanon, and from the great river, the Euphrates—all the Hittite country—to the great sea on the west."* In God's original promise to Abram in Genesis 13:17, He says, *"Go, walk through the length and breadth of the land, for I am giving it to you."* As we will see in the pages that follow, God gives specifics and directives in order to secure the fullness of life for His people in the generations that would follow.

INSTRUCTIONS GIVEN TO JOSHUA

We are all familiar with the biblical account of Joshua and his people marching around the city of Jericho. (Joshua 6) This marching went on for six days then on the seventh day they marched around the city seven times. (Joshua 6:14–15) It is a dramatic story that ends in the total collapse of Jericho based on the detailed instructions given by God.

> By following the detailed instructions of the Lord, He gives us access into the land addressing both the seen and unseen issues that are at work.

In Joshua 18, clear instructions are given to the people for the purposes of accessing and dividing the land into the hands of the various tribes. *"As the men started on their way to map out the land, Joshua instructed them, 'Go and make a survey and write a description of it. Then return to me, and I will cast lots for you here at Shiloh here in the presence of the Lord.' So the men left and went through the land. They wrote its description on a scroll, town by town, in seven parts and returned to Joshua in the camp at Shiloh."* (Joshua 18:8–9) Undoubtedly, both Joshua and Caleb had vivid memories of what had happened nearly forty years earlier. This account is found in Numbers 13 and 14 in which God had given instructions to the spies to go and explore the Promised Land. Although this reconnaissance was undertaken, ten of the spies fell into the fear of man due to the size of the giants they encountered. They had obeyed the instructions to explore the land, but clearly had not taken everything into proper account. The implication is that by following the detailed instructions of the Lord, He gives us access into the land addressing both the seen and unseen issues that are at work. By physically positioning ourselves upon the land, God is able to instruct us accordingly.

IN MORE RECENT TIMES

In the early 1900s, the Salvation Army began the practice of marching through the streets of London with musical instruments. This, in fact, was simply a new wineskin of a Godly instruction asking his people to inherit the land. The practice of taking praise and prayer into public streets later gave rise to what became known as "March for Jesus". Even to this day, people have begun to recognize the value and importance and strategy of placing their feet upon the very land into which God has called them to live and work.

On Saturday, July 14th, 2012, an estimated 1 million people marched in São Paulo, Brazil bringing together Christians of all denominations. Although the ministry of "March for Jesus", per se, does not exist as an organization any longer, the practice of the people of God taking to the streets continues on a global basis.[5]

During my years in parish ministry, our leaders and intercessors would walk the length and width of our areas of pastoral responsibility within the city limits on a regular basis. We learned about issues we had not been aware of earlier that affected the people in our pastoral care. In all three of our residential ministries in England, Scotland and Canada, we experienced many breakthroughs in our church life that was a direct result of walking the land and "beating the bounds".

2 Corinthians 4:4 states: *"The god of this age has blinded the minds of unbelievers, so that they cannot see the light of the gospel of the glory of Christ, who is the image of God."* We began to learn that there were spiritual issues collectively blinding people to the existence of our church. To the degree we walked the land within our parish boundaries, to the same degree we began to see breakthrough taking place in the corporate mindset of our areas of responsibility. Subsequently significant breakthroughs of ministry took place. Often we would hear people who began to visit our church for the first time saying, "We've never seen this church here before!" Clearly their ability to see had changed quite significantly. (Isaiah 32:3)

I was, for a period of time, Chaplain to the board of "March for Jesus" in Canada, and many times we received dramatic accounts of conversions, healings, changes in the lives of people, significant breakthroughs in churches and deepened relationships between the church and the city. This occurred in a variety of city templates both in Canada and overseas. Over the years we have learned that distinct change can take place upon the land, and within cities, and certainly within churches and businesses, when the people in their defined areas of responsibility walk the land with Godly posture and undertake specified instructions within the parameters established by the leadership.

WHY DOES GOD SET BOUNDARIES FOR HIS PEOPLE?

This question needs to be answered in order to understand something significant and compelling concerning the character of God. Too many people liken Him to a killjoy or some form of slave master wielding a large whip over his people. We need to examine the nature of God when it comes to the boundaries and parameters He has set for His people.

In their book *Boundaries*, Dr. Henry Cloud and Dr. John Townsend[6] give an in–depth study on physical, mental, emotional, and spiritual boundaries. As mentioned on the back cover of their book, *"Having*

Scripture reveals that the boundaries God establishes for us exist in order for His work and His blessings to be revealed and released.

clear boundaries is essential to a healthy, balanced lifestyle. A boundary is a personal property line that marks those things for which we are responsible. Boundaries define who we are and who we are not." They continue on this note by saying, *"The concept of boundaries comes from the very nature of God. God defines Himself as a distinct, separate being, and He is responsible for Himself. He defines and takes responsibility for His personality by telling us what He thinks, feels, plans, allows, will not allow, likes, and dislikes."* (page 32)

Scripture reveals that the boundaries God establishes for us exist in order for His work and His blessings to be revealed and released. However, living within His boundaries requires our agreeing to certain parameters He has determined for us. Even Jesus prayed with this in mind when He said, *"...not my will, but yours be done."* (Luke 22:42) Jesus modelled this principle for us even when He faced death by showing that, in yielding to God the responsibility of working out our own direction in life, we receive the life that *He* has chosen for us. If we choose to follow God's plan and purpose (Jeremiah 29:11) then our reactions, our habits, our attitudes, all weave together to form a beautiful mosaic in which all things work together for good for those who love and trust Him. (Romans 8:28)

As Cloud and Townsend reveal throughout the chapters of their book, boundaries enable us to recognize and practice the type of lifestyle God intends for us. It requires discipline. It requires an acceptance that the boundaries of God actually yield freedom, not restriction. Putting it another way, true freedom requires our agreement to certain restraints, guidelines and boundaries. Through Scripture, we learn that God gives boundaries to protect us from moral and spiritual calamity at a personal, relational, emotional and practical level. This is how we experience the abundant life that Jesus promises.

How then can we define the word *boundary*? The Shorter Oxford English Dictionary[7] defines boundary as "*that which serves to indicate the limits of anything; the limit itself*". The dictionary defines cricket as a game in which the boundaries determine the enclosure for the cricket match. It defines a boundary line as an established line marking the limits of a town or estate. Further, it gives an example of a boundary rider in Australia as one who rides round the fences of a station and repairs them when broken. If, therefore, we could develop a working definition for the word *boundary* it would be seen as a limit or an edge or a property line. Often one's property is determined by walls, hedges or even signs that represent ownership. As we will see in Scripture, there are privileges, responsibilities and expectations that go hand in hand with the ownership and stewardship of property.

There are certain things that God allows and certain things He does not allow. When Adam and Eve ate the fruit of the tree of knowledge in order to be like God knowing good and evil (Genesis 3:5), this resulted in all future generations experiencing death. In other words, God set the boundary and, when man violated the boundary, he had to endure the consequences that followed.

What is intriguing about God is that He has given us freedom of choice and He does not violate our boundaries. Revelation 3:20 depicts Jesus standing at the door of our heart and knocking but will only enter when we give Him permission to do so. Therefore, a person has the choice to live life God's way, or in his own way. If it is the latter, we can violate our own boundaries, our personal boundaries can be violated by others, or we may violate the boundaries of other people.

We learn from the nature of God that the foundation of boundaries is love, but this can be forfeited or become subject to deception. God originally gave boundaries to His people because He loves them. However He also expects us to take responsibility for the boundaries He has determined since this is what yields the fullness of His purpose in our lives. Ever since the fall of man in Genesis 3, however, people have

Boundaries are centered on the restoration of freedom that God wants for His people in order to live life with a divine purpose.

wanted to be in control of their own lives without any reference to God.

On one occasion while I was flying to a ministry venue, I was passing the time by watching an inflight TV movie. Prior to the movie a brief infomercial appeared on the screen with these words: *"You are about to experience a life where there are greater possibilities than there are barriers. A life where the world is one big country waiting to be explored and enjoyed. One where you will do more—see more—live more. This is life without boundaries."*[8]

This advertisement was sponsored by a well–known financial institution. In reality, while it sounds good, it is a statement on man's desire wanting to live life his way on his conditions. It is a statement for the twenty–first century lifestyle. God has given us freedom of choice, yet at the same time requires us to be responsible and accountable in what we do. He expects us to be good stewards of our feelings, attitudes, behaviors, choices, limits, talents, thoughts, desires, loves and values. Therefore all of these and other areas of responsibility need to be understood through the lens of Galatians 5:1—*"It is for freedom that Christ has set us free. Stand firm, then, and do not let yourselves be burdened again by a yoke of slavery."* If Jesus indeed did die to set us free from the consequences and restrictions of sin, the devil, and the systems of the world, then we need to recognize that boundaries are centered on the restoration of freedom that God wants for His people in order to live life with a divine purpose.

In Deuteronomy 2:4 we read these words—*"....You are about to pass through the territory of your brothers the descendants of Esau, who live in Seir. They will be afraid of you, but be very careful."* God's boundaries are signs and indicators that restrict us from going the wrong way, but enable us to go the right way without wasting time on detours! What is interesting about the book of Deuteronomy, which means "repetition of the law", is that after forty years waiting for a generation of unbelief to disappear, the Israelites were now about to enter Canaan. However before doing so, Moses wanted to remind them of their history, and all that God had done for them, and all the various laws that were essential for them to maintain as God's chosen people, ***if*** they were to obtain the fullness of life in the way God had intended originally.

Continuing in Deuteronomy 2:5, God gives further indicators concerning His boundaries for them. *"Do not provoke them to war, for I will not give you any of their land, not even enough to put your foot on. I have given Esau the hill country of Seir as his own. You are to pay them in silver for the food you eat and the water you drink. The Lord your God has blessed you in all the work of your hands. He has watched over your journey through this vast desert. These forty years the Lord your God has been with you, and you have not lacked anything."* (Deuteronomy 2: 5–7) In the verses that follow, God indicates who His people are to befriend, who their enemies are and who they will need to defeat in battle.

Repeatedly, as long as His people would stay within the boundaries He has prepared for them, His promise to them was repeated time and time again—*"Do not be afraid of them; the Lord your God himself will fight for you."* (Deuteronomy 3:22) Deuteronomy 4:40 reveals the heart of God for His people—*"Keep his decrees and commands, which I am giving you today, so that it may go well with you and your children after you and that you may live long in the land the Lord your God gives you for all time."* Moses then explains God's law and commandments for His people and ends with these words—*"So be careful to do what the Lord your God has commanded you; do not turn aside to the right or to the left. Walk in all the way that the Lord your God has commanded you, so that you may live and prosper and prolong your days in the land that you will possess."* (Deuteronomy 5:32–33) That is the heart of God for His people! That is God's intent for His people! That is God's destiny for His people!

God created land before He created us, and our responsibility is to steward the land He entrusted to us.

God continues to give further revelation and depth to the promises He makes for His people—*"But remember the Lord your God, for it is he who gives you the ability to produce wealth, and so confirms his covenant, which he swore to your forefathers, as it is today."* (Deuteronomy 8:18)

Then He goes even further with these words: *"If you carefully observe all these commands I am giving you to follow—to love the Lord your God, to walk in all his ways and to hold fast to him—then the Lord will drive out all these nations before you, and you will dispossess nations larger and stronger than you. Every place where you set your foot will be yours; your territory will extend from the desert to Lebanon, and from the Euphrates River to the western sea. No man will be able to stand against you. The Lord your God, as he promised you, will put the terror and fear of you on the whole land, wherever you go."* (Deuteronomy 11:22–25)

Profound promises from a loving God! However, there were also consequences if man chose to live life in his own way and did not want "loving restrictions" that he might believe were limiting him. (Deuteronomy 11:28 & 28:15–68) It's our choice. But the benefits of understanding and implementing God's boundaries in our lives yield the full resources of the kingdom of God in our midst, lasting for generations.

UNDERSTANDING AND IMPLEMENTING GOD'S BOUNDARIES

As I shared in the book *Releasing Heaven on Earth,*[9] God created land before He created us, and our responsibility is to steward the land He entrusted to us.

This land is represented by our cities, our areas of work and worship, our homes and our families. Indeed it stretches from the role of the individual right up to the role of a nation. Scripture teaches us about the cause and effect of sin upon the land, and how land can be healed. (2 Chronicles 7:14) We now turn to one of the most fascinating and overlooked principles in Scripture concerning God's teaching on boundary lines and boundary stones that affect us all—whether an individual or a nation.

> In Deuteronomy 19:14 we read: *"Do not move your neighbor's boundary stone set up by your predecessors in the inheritance you receive in the land the Lord your God is giving you to possess."* Similarly in Deuteronomy 27:17— *"Cursed is the man who moves his neighbor's boundary stone..."* Proverbs 22:28 states it this way: *"Do not move an ancient boundary stone set up by your forefathers,"* which is further explained in Proverbs 23:10–11, *"Do not move an ancient boundary stone or encroach on the fields of the fatherless, for their Defender is strong; he will take up their case against you."* Then the prophet Hosea would offer these words—*"Judah's leaders are like those who move boundary stones. I will pour out my wrath on them like a flood of water."* (Hosea 5:10)

These verses all indicate something tangible and urgent concerning God's relationship with his people. With reference to Deuteronomy 19:14, *The Bible Knowledge Commentary*[10] explains that Moses placed this law concerning the boundary stone in between the teaching he gives on the legislation over cities of refuge (vs.1–13) and the false witnesses (15–21), and then states: "In those days...moving a neighbor's boundary stone was equivalent to stealing his property."

Clark's Commentary on the Bible[11] explains this in more detail. The inference is that no ancient landmark is to be removed. *"Before the extensive use of fences, landed property was marked out by stones or posts, set up so as to ascertain the divisions of family estates. It was easy to remove one of these landmarks, and set it in a different place, and thus the dishonest man enlarged his own estate by contracting that of his neighbor." Clarke also remarks that to the Romans, these landmarks were held to be very sacred and that various levels of punishment would be levied upon those changing such a landmark, and if there was evil intent on the part of slaves who changed those landmarks, then they were put to death.* The issue is one of theft, both of property but also of inheritance and stewardship and the responsibility of ownership in maintaining those landmarks.

On this same note Coffman's Commentary[12] points out that the whole issue has to do with the right of property. *"We stress people rights versus property rights. But the glaring truth is that there are never any PEOPLE rights unless also there are PROPERTY rights. Property is the ability to maintain and support life, and there has never been discovered by any human society any way to get rid of property rights... The true religion has always recognized the rights of private property, with the precautionary truth that all property is 'owned' by the children of God as 'stewards of God's grace', and that they are responsible for its use in some manner pleasing to God."*

If we are removing a boundary stone, it means we are simply replacing or displacing something God originally established for His people in order to promise them both protection and provision. If we extend our boundary stones or markers into somebody else's property, that is the same as theft. This incurs God's wrath and anger. This renders us vulnerable to the systems of life in that new territory in which we have neither protection nor understanding. It means we have belligerently and deliberately made a decision apart from God's direction and/or permission for us. This can also mean entering into new areas of knowledge, and worship and praxis that are not part of His "territory" or "custodianship" or "stewardship" for our lives.

In terms of deception, this is how the Church and society today are so quickly led into new areas of thought and practice. It feels good, it appeals to our humanism. In fact, if we look at Deuteronomy 27:17 again, *"Cursed is the man who moves his neighbor's boundary stone,"* we see we can be entering into unknown and dangerous territory. This, in fact, becomes a "new neighborhood" that has been established as "off limits" for us.

Little wonder in Numbers 13 and Joshua 18 that God asked His people to undertake due diligence and careful research before entering into the new land ***He*** had prepared for them. Even then, God offered clarity concerning the issues they would face. In Numbers 13 they dismissed God's wisdom while in Joshua 18 they were able to occupy the new territory because they did so under God's jurisdiction.

Deuteronomy 32:8 indicates that *"when the Most High gave the nations their inheritance, when he divided all mankind, he set up boundaries for the peoples..."* and the rest of Deuteronomy indicates the manner in which He established His portions for His people. He gave them nourishment and protection and direction so long as they took His words to heart. (Deuteronomy 32:46–47) These were not just idle words but rather they contained the promise of His life in them and *"By them you will live long in the land you are crossing the Jordan to possess."* (Deuteronomy 32:47)

Once the Church jettisons the foundations of faith received from the early Church, and develops new doctrine and expression through revelation and experience, we are in dire danger of removing God's boundary stones—the very foundations that have kept us safe and secure in accord with **His** promise of **His** life working in and through us.

A further reason why God gave a law against removing the ancient landmarks was due to the fact that the inheritances of tribes and families were distinguished through these God–given markers. Joshua 15:12b indicates that the boundaries which were already referred to in the earlier chapters of Joshua and those in the chapters to follow, are the boundaries that have been established around the people of Judah, clan by clan.

The New Living Translation of Proverbs 22:28 states: *"Do not move an ancient boundary stone set up by your fathers."* In other words do not cheat your neighbor by moving the ancient boundary markers set up by previous generations. When we examine this verse along with Proverbs 23:10 and in light of Deuteronomy 27:17, we are actually invoking a curse upon ourselves by going beyond God's established perimeters. Putting it another way, we are removing ourselves from under the cover of God's protection and we are also endangering the lives of those whose land we are entering through theft and disobedience.

When His rest, His destiny and His resting place is established on our land, it will become attractive to others and draw people to His presence.

Is this being legalistic in our understanding of God? If we do not have a healthy worldview which takes into account the spiritual issues that affect what goes on in society and upon the land, then in fact, we are entering into spiritual realms for which we do not have adequate protection. We shall see shortly why this is probably the case. If we took time to review all of Numbers 34, Joshua 13–19 and then Ezekiel 47:13–22, we would see that God's perspective on physical boundaries cannot be overlooked or ignored. Ezekiel 47:21–23 gives further insight: *"'You are to distribute this land among yourselves according to the tribes of Israel. You are to allot it as an inheritance for yourselves* ***and for the aliens*** *(emphasis mine) who have settled among you and who have children. You are to consider them as native–born Israelites; along with you they are to be allotted an inheritance among with the tribes of Israel. In whatever tribe the alien settles, there you are to give him his inheritance,' declares the Sovereign Lord."*

To the degree we bring our area of responsibility—our stewardship for the Lord—into relationship with God, then it becomes a place of refuge and work and life for those whom God calls into our territory. As referred to in *Releasing Heaven on Earth,*[13] the land reflects God's opinion, and when His rest, His destiny and His resting place is established on our land, it will become attractive to others and draw people to His presence (John 12:32).

Therefore, in all these Scriptures we have looked at so far concerning God's boundary lines and stones for his people, there is both a geographical and spiritual perspective in the manner He gives protection, direction and provision, while at the same time securing the inheritance of His people who dwell within the parameters of His destiny for them.

In the next chapter we will see what happens when we try to extend our territory into somebody else's property. This is something that can be done either wittingly and unwittingly, whether in the Church, in business, or even at the level of a nation. In Job 24:2 we read, *"Men move boundary stones; [and consequently] they pasture flocks they have stolen."* As we will see shortly, when we steal other people's property and destiny, we also receive their problems!

There is a reason why God gives such clarity on these matters. It is out of His love and concern for His people, and not out of any divine legalistic pleasure. In this vein, however, Proverbs 15:25 gives us a sober warning—*"The Lord tears down the proud man's house [i.e. he who establishes his own boundaries]—but he keeps the widow's boundaries intact."*

The well–known adage warns that pride comes before a man's fall. Is this not the same for churches, businesses, cities, and even nations? Ponder these sobering words from Isaiah 10:12–13—*"When the Lord has finished all his work against Mount Zion and Jerusalem, he will say, 'I will punish the King of Assyria for the willful pride of his heart and the haughty look in his eyes.' For he says: 'By the strength of my hand I have done this, and by my wisdom, because I have understanding. I removed the boundaries of nations, I plundered their treasures; like a mighty one I subdued their kings.'"*

Simply put, the Lord punishes all levels of leadership for willful pride of heart and He can remove the protection and security of nations and have their treasures and provisions taken by others. This was the solemn reminder that God gave through Joshua before the people of God entered the Promised Land.

> *"Do not let this Book of the Law depart from your mouth; meditate on it day and night, that you may be careful to do everything written in it. Then you will be prosperous and successful. Have I not commanded you? Be strong and courageous. Do not be terrified; do*

not be discouraged, for the Lord your God will be with you wherever you go." (Joshua 1:8–9)

The Book of the Law—the Word of God—would become the most secure boundary line possible for the people of God in all that lay ahead of them. God was saying in these words that His desire was for His people to have abundant life and health and safety and increase, but only if they held fast to the Word of the Lord who would guide and direct them. How interesting and how challenging are the words of Deuteronomy 4:2—*"Do not add to what I command you and do not subtract from it, but keep the commands of the Lord your God that I give you."* Similarly, Revelation 22:18–19 states, *"I warn everyone who hears the words of the prophecy of this book: If anyone adds anything to them, God will add to him the plagues described in this book. And if anyone takes words away from this book of prophecy, God will take away from him his share in the tree of life and in the holy city, which are described in this book."* Simply put, the Old and the New Testaments both confirm the same principle that the Word of God is life. Staying within His boundary lines releases His grace and authority within our lives delivering His promises of provision, blessing and protection. (Deuteronomy 28:1–14)

When we live within the security of the Lord and do not go ahead of His counsel and direction, then He takes on the enemies that we face.

In all probability, this is what is inferred in Psalm 16:6, *"The boundary lines have fallen for me in pleasant places; surely I have a delightful inheritance."* In the verses that follow the Psalmist indicates that within these boundary lines, he receives God's counsel, God's instruction, God's presence and the protection of God's right hand. This is why the heart of the Psalmist is glad and his tongue rejoices in all that God has done in him and through him. (Psalm 16:7–11) Our boundary lines will always be pleasant (sweet) when we live within the markers God has prepared for us.

All of Psalm 78 is an amazing testimony of the provision and protection that God gives to His people and in verses 54 and 55 we read these words, *"Thus he brought them to the border of his holy land, to the hill country his right hand had taken. He drove out nations before them and allotted their lands to them as an inheritance; he settled the tribes of Israel in their homes."* Here we see that when we live within the security of the Lord and do not go ahead of His counsel and direction, then *He* takes on the enemies that we face—it is not something that we have to do in our own strength. The enemies and challenges, of course, would be those issues that are the fiery arrows the enemy sends in our direction to try and interfere with our God–given destiny.

DIGGING DEEPER

With all this in mind, we now need to examine the issue of borders and boundaries and boundary stones at a deeper level. Without examining every reference to these terms in Scripture (and there are many!), we have seen that the issue of boundary lines goes back to the Garden of Eden.

As we see in Deuteronomy 10:13, God's boundaries are set up for our wellbeing. They help us to stay within His will. As Psalm 36:1 states, *"... An oracle is within my heart concerning the sinfulness of the wicked; there is no fear of God before his eyes."* Having the fear of the Lord in our lives is not an issue of timidity and apprehension concerning God—rather it is having a sense of awe and reverence of who God is and what He wants to do in and through us, a desire to be obedient to all the Lord has taught us, and a willingness to resist evil at all costs. When we do not have the fear of the Lord in our lives, we will not understand the peace that He wants us to experience even in the midst of tribulation. (Romans 3:17–18)

Understanding the security of God's boundaries in our lives enables us to appreciate the significance of John 16:33—*"I have told you these things, so that in me you may have peace. In this world you will have*

His boundaries are a means by which His law and purpose for us come to life and activate His purpose in and through us.

trouble. But take heart! I have overcome the world." Therefore, God's boundaries protect us from evil, enable us to stay away from sin, and secure our comfort and safety. As Micah 6:8 would indicate, God requires that we *"...act justly and to love mercy and to walk humbly..."* How fascinating that in the next verse we read these words, *"Listen! The Lord is calling to the city—and to fear your name is wisdom—Heed the rod and the One who appointed it."* (Micah 6:9)

Therefore, His boundaries are a means by which His law and purpose for us come to life and activate His purpose in and through us. His motive is not to build a negative fence around us, but rather to release His love from within us.

He is the God of boundaries. Job 26:10 reminds us: *"He marks out the horizon on the face of the waters for a boundary between light and darkness."* He determines the boundaries between heaven and earth—*"There is a time for everything and a season for every activity under Heaven."* (Ecclesiastes 3:1) These boundaries and directives provide perimeters of predictability and sustainability for our lives, giving us confidence that we can trust in His reliability. He is, after all, the God of the impossible (Luke 1:37). He defines the boundaries of the sea and the foundations of the earth (Job 38:8–11; Psalm 104:9; Proverbs 8:29).

In Jeremiah 5:22, God is quite candid in what He says concerning himself—*"'Should you not fear me?' declares the Lord. 'Should you not tremble in my presence? I made the sand a boundary for the sea, an everlasting barrier it cannot cross. The waves may roll, but they cannot prevail; they may roar, but they cannot cross it.'"* He continues in verse 24 by saying, *"...Let us fear the Lord our God, who gives autumn and spring rains in season, who assures us of the regular weeks of harvest."* In fact, in Genesis 8:22, God promises that the seasons of life will continue, *"As long as the earth endures, seedtime and harvest, cold and heat, summer and winter, day and night will never cease."*

His boundaries at times are boundaries of discipline (Psalm 94:12), but in the end He disciplines us purely for the purpose of our sharing in His holiness (Hebrews 12:7–11). If we stray beyond His boundaries, we will normally suffer the consequences, but He allows this in order to bring us back into our correct relationship with Him. For this reason, Paul reminds us that we have the mind of Christ at work within us (1 Corinthians 2:16) and we are not to *"...conform any longer to the pattern of this world, but be transformed by the renewing of your mind... to test and approve what God's will is—his good, pleasing and perfect will."* (Romans 12:2)

SEEING WITH A WORLDVIEW LENS

One of our major challenges today is the issue of worldview. If we hold to a worldview that fully understands the spirit realm, then we will understand why God cautioned us about going beyond His borders. A western–based worldview is subject to dualism in which the spiritual and physical realms are separated. The issue of dualism has existed long before the coming of Christ, and over many generations has influenced culture, education, morals and ethics, as well as religion, global economics, politics, marketing and industry—indeed family and society as a whole.

Nations, cities, businesses, churches, and of course individuals, endanger themselves spiritually if they change their boundaries and go beyond the parameters God has established for them. In all probability, this lies behind Paul's thinking in 2 Corinthians 10:13–15—*"We, however, will not boast beyond proper limits, but will confine our boasting to the field God has assigned to us, a field that reaches even to you... Our hope is that as your faith continues to grow, our area of activity among you will greatly expand."* This is a fascinating verse to compare in various translations.

> For example, the New English Bible[14] says, *"With us there will be no attempt to boast beyond our proper sphere; and our sphere is determined by the limit God laid down for us..."*
>
> The Amplified Version[15] says, *"We, on the other hand, will not boast beyond our legitimate province and proper limit, but will keep within the limits (of our commission which) God has allotted us as our measuring line and which reaches and includes even you."*
>
> The Common English Bible[16] says, *"We won't take pride in anything more than what is appropriate. Let's look at the boundaries of our work area that God has assigned to us. It is an area that includes you."*

The Greek word in question here that is translated as measure or sphere or boundary is *metron*. This indicates an area of authority with logistical ramifications.

It is essential that we understand this sphere or metron at work within us as well as the physical metron of our responsibility. For example in Acts 19:13–16, there were some who were trying to undertake deliverance in the name of Jesus Christ, but the evil spirit answered, *"Jesus I know, and I know about Paul, but who are you? Then the man who had the evil spirit jumped on them and overpowered them all..."* (Acts 19:15–16) As Proverbs 21:16 so aptly puts it, *"A man who strays from the path of understanding comes to rest in the company of the dead."*

This is why it is urgent that we understand the words of Jeremiah 6:16—*"This is what the Lord says: Stand at the crossroads and look; ask for the ancient paths, ask where the good way is, and walk in it, and you will find rest for your souls..."* We will examine in further detail, the principle behind 2 Corinthians 10:13–15 since there are times when God asks us to extend our boundary lines into new territory. In the meantime, as Jeremiah 6:16 reminds us, we are to ensure that our work and life and ministry is maintained and determined by the ancient landmarks that God established for us in the beginning.

IMPORTANCE OF BOUNDARIES

Clearly we have seen there are principles which form a non–negotiable part of God's ongoing covenant in our lives and which convey essential spiritual principles for our life and destiny. They establish God's parameters as blessing and safety and protection (Deuteronomy 28:1–14; Matthew 5:17–18). Indeed, Matthew 5:17–18 is a timely reminder that, although we live in the era of the New Testament, the parameters of the Law and prophets are still our parameters today. Indeed, *"... not the smallest letter, not the least stroke of a pen, will by any means disappear from the Law until everything is accomplished..."* (Matthew 5:18)

As seen in 2 Corinthians 10:13–15, boundaries protect us from trespassing. If we go beyond our borders or our limits, we can become vulnerable to the spiritual issues in that new region. I referred earlier to the book *Transformed! People – Cities – Nations*[17] which was based on research undertaken in order to determine why revivals come to an early conclusion. There were 10 main reasons why this premature ending takes place but, if stewarded correctly, these ten reasons would instead become keys for sustaining the presence and work of God in our midst. Similarly, if we "steward our boundaries", what we receive in return is profound:

- Boundaries protect our identity;
- Boundaries authenticate our ministry with integrity and authenticity;
- Boundaries secure our geography (safety and protection);
- Boundaries establish our strengths and guard our weaknesses;
- Boundaries maintain Godly order in church and society and also sustain essential foundations;
- Boundaries guard correct doctrine and warn against heresy;
- Boundaries authenticate the purity of the supernatural and alert us to the seduction of unholy/unauthorized fire (Leviticus 10:1);
- Boundaries maintain honor within nations;
- Boundaries ensure correct ethics within commerce and trade.

Proverbs 10:2 offers us some penetrating words—*"Ill–gotten treasures are of no value, but righteousness delivers from death..."* Proverbs 13:11 goes on to state, *"Dishonest money dwindles away, but he who gathers money little by little makes it grow."* Further teaching comes from Proverbs 21:6 in these words—*"A fortune made by a lying tongue is a fleeting vapor and a deadly* snare."

In Luke Chapter 3 when John the Baptist preached his sermon on repentance the crowd, the tax collectors and even the military asked Him how they should respond to what he had taught. Quite clearly He indicated they were to share, not to collect more taxes than was required, and not to extort money and accuse people falsely. Little wonder why today God is shaking almost every level of business and commerce in society!

Boundaries allow for the expansion of what we steward so that in due course we can extend the Kingdom of God through our life and work.

NEGLECTING GOD'S BOUNDARIES

As we have seen so far this is a serious subject from God's perspective. When His boundaries are neglected:

- This results in pride and arrogance;
- This releases the spirits of law and entitlement;
- This provides the enemy with foothold leverage;
- This exposes our vulnerability in both spiritual and physical realms;
- This removes God's protection and canopy of cover from our lives;
- This allows nations to exploit nations;
- This results in leaders proclaiming autonomy and dictatorship and creates double standards;
- This results in extortion and usury and exploitation;
- This removes justice and brings injustice;
- This introduces humanism and universalism;
- This results in deception and God–sent delusion (2 Thessalonians 2:11–12).

WHEN A NATION FORGETS GOD

Erwin W Lutzer wrote some very sobering thoughts in his book *When a Nation Forgets God.*[18] When we forego, jettison or neglect the boundaries God has established for us whether at the level of a nation or an individual, then we will find that the following issues arise: the raw use of power – eroticism – arbitrary judicial rulings – the morality of personal pragmatism – false economy which leads to a nation in debt – a developing scenario in which the children become owned by the state (making the future of home–schooling somewhat questionable) – cheap grace in that Christ may be the Head of the Church but the Kaiser (Caesar) is the head of the political sphere which teaches that allegiance to God is best demonstrated by allegiance to the state. History has much to teach us!

SOME CONCLUSIONS

Surveyors regularly leave brightly colored flags just outside city and land boundaries. This is readily seen when a highway extension is taking place and such flags can be seen on trees or on pegs driven into the ground. These boundary markers are informational reference points indicating what will be taking place in the future. Various forms of legal and financial obligations are usually undertaken before those markers become actual official boundaries which signify the extension of a property or boundary line. Normally the terrain needs to be prepared accordingly. This requires the removal of impediments and obstacles to what will take place one day. In the meantime, the present boundary markers and stones signify ownership, occupancy and even authority.

We have already seen what happens when we ignore the signs and signals God gives to His people when He is trying to get our attention. We have looked at the various ways in which we are being shaken at literally every level of life in this day and age. It would appear that God is clearly giving His people a **wake–up call**. We have begun to explore the whole issue of deception and how and why it is affecting the church in the twenty–first century. Having just reviewed the whole issue of boundary lines and boundary stones, perhaps now there is clarity as to why God may be establishing boundary markers for us all in these coming days. We have much to address before the return of Christ, and based on what we have seen so far if we do not respond accordingly, then we may see an increase in...

- Controlled economics and an emerging currency that may affect every nation.
- Controlled buying and selling through institutions such as banking systems, requiring most, if not all, of our most confidential details.
- Control of life through such basic components of life as healthcare and social systems requiring full disclosure of personal details.
- Control of governments by other governments. The present situation in Europe possibly is foreshadowing what the book of Revelation says will take place. It is highly possible that a 'United States of Europe' may well emerge along with its first President.
- Controlled food supplies—panic buying could take place at an increasing level. Already in the United States and in parts of Europe, people are beginning to 'store up' in case a crisis comes in the next few months or years.
- Control of religious freedom, especially if the church leans more on the fear of man than upon the fear of God.

We now need to examine the implications and applications of what we have studied so far, as well as the manner in which God is positioning His church within the global arena for such a time as this.

---

1. *Complete Jewish Bible* Translator: David H Stern, Jewish New Testament Publications, Inc., Clarksville, Maryland USA, 1998 ISBN 0 19 529751 2
2. *Amplified Bible* (AMP), Published by The Lockman Foundation, 1987 Printing version as used on Bible Gateway; www.biblegateway.com
3. *New American Standard Version*, The Lockman Foundation; 1995 Printing as used on Bible Gateway Website www.revival–library.org
4. Bounds as described in Wikipedia – Wikipedia.org/wiki/Beating_the_bounds

5. Source from *Christian Post World* article – by Anugrah Kumar, Christian Post Contributor – July 15th, 2012 – By Anugrah Kumar, Christian Post Contributor – www.christianpost.com
6. *Boundaries* Authors: Dr. Henry Cloud and Dr. John Townsend – Zondervan Publishing House, Grand Rapids, Michigan 49530, 1992, ISBN 0 310 20974 9
7. *Shorter Oxford English Dictionary* – Wikipedia – www.wikipedia.org
8. Air Canada in–flight infomercial, 2011 – HSBC
9. *Releasing Heaven on Earth* Author: Alistair P. Petrie – Republished July 2008 – Sovereign World Ltd. ISBN 97818 52404 819
10. *The Bible Knowledge Commentary* Authors: John F Walvoord and Roy B Zuck – Published by Victor Books – a division of Scripture Press Publications, Inc., Wheaton Il 1985 ISBN 0 88207 813 5 (page 298)
11. *Clarke's Commentary On The Bible* Author: Adam Clarke From Google Search – *Commentary on Deuteronomy 19:14*. "The Adam Clarke Commentary" http://www.studylight.org/com/acc/view.1832
12. *Coffman Commentaries on the Bible* Author: James Burton – Deuteronomy 19 www.studylight.org
13. *Releasing Heaven on Earth* Author: Alistair P. Petrie – Republished July 2008 – Sovereign World Ltd. ISBN 97818 52404 819
14. *The New English Bible*, New York, Oxford University Press, 1971
15. *Amplified Bible* (AMP), Published by The Lockman Foundation, 1987 Printing version as used on Bible Gateway; www.biblegateway.com
16. *Common English Bible*, (CEB), 2011, Bible Gateway – http://www.biblegateway.com
17. *Transformed! People–Cities–Nations* Author: Alistair P Petrie – Republished July 2008 – Sovereign World Ltd. ISBN 97818 52404 826
18. *When A Nation Forgets God: 7 Lessons We Must Learn from Nazi Germany* Author: Erwin W Lutzer; Moody Publishers, 2010, Moody Publishers Chicago, Illinois ISBN 97808 02446 565

5

GOD'S BOUNDARIES—*Implications and Applications*

The repeated theme throughout Scripture is that when the people of God repent and return to the Lord following a season of willful sin, then He is gracious and compassionate and He will relent from sending calamity. We learn from Scripture that God has love for His land and for His people, *"Then the Lord will be jealous for his land and take pity on his people."* (Joel 2:18) The evidence of the Old Testament is that God longs to bless His people with His presence and His provision. This theme is carried on into the New Testament. A substantial amount of the teaching found in the parables of the Kingdom of God reveal the heart of God in wanting to release His blessing and purpose in the lives of His people. In *Releasing Heaven on Earth,*[1] I indicate that there are well over 1700 verses in Scripture concerning the relationship of God, man and land. Land reflects God's opinion on what is taking place in the lives and stewardship of His people!

In considering all that we have seen so far in these first four chapters, we now need to examine further the implications upon land when the boundaries God assigned to nations and people are broken, stolen or changed. We also need to see the implications for us today in the

> The desire of the Lord is always to release His peace and destiny and provision in the lives of His people.

twenty–first century Church. A general teaching throughout the Old Testament is that when the people of God sin, then foreign nations are allowed to invade the land and march across the borders. (Micah 5:6) The desire of the Lord is always to release His peace and destiny and provision in the lives of His people—*"He grants peace to your borders and satisfies you with the finest of wheat."* (Psalm 147:14) When the people of God are in relationship with Him, the expression of Isaiah 60:18 reveals the heart of God—*"No longer will violence be heard in your land, nor ruin or destruction within your borders, but you will call your walls Salvation and your gates Praise."*

It can also be argued that God does want to extend His boundary lines beyond what He originally gave to His people since this is part of His witness and testimony through those who walk in covenant with him. Isaiah 54:2–3 would indicate this principle, *"Enlarge the place of your tent, stretch your tent curtains wide, do not pull back; lengthen your cords, strengthen your stakes. For you will spread out to the right and to the left; your descendants will dispossess nations and settle in their desolate cities."* In modern times, this is most likely the best way to describe transformation templates of cities and territories that are still experiencing authentic revival in which the presence of God has begun to permeate all the various institutions and fabric of life in those areas. In the last few years alone, there have been many templates of transformational revival that have taken place once the residential people in those respective areas addressed the issues on the land and in society that had become an offence to God. The Sentinel Group (www.sentinelgroup.org) is a research ministry that provides much evidence on this subject.

We can view in more contemporary history what has happened when boundary stones have been changed, thus affecting the lives of those who live in nations and cities. Again, Job 24:2 reflects on this issue, *"Men move boundary stones; they pasture flocks they have stolen."* Similarly, in Hosea 5:10 we read, *"Judah's leaders are like those who move boundary stones. I will pour out my wrath on them like a flood of water."* Let us now turn to some of the implications that we can view through the lens of modern history.

THE IMPLICATIONS OF MOVING BOUNDARIES

Historically, there are very few nations whose boundaries have not at one time or another been moved through varying circumstances. Let's consider some of the consequences.

When a nation has its boundary lines removed, changed or extended through a treaty or during war, does this have an ongoing cause and effect upon that nation? Scripture teaches us that a city and a nation actually have their foundations influenced through the people involved in the founding, growth and development of that nation. This can result in strengths and weaknesses that develop within the corporate life of the nation or city depending on the circumstances of the people involved. In 1 Corinthians 3:10–12, Paul uses the word "foundation" with reference to one's ministry. And yet the same word is used as the "foundation" of human personality and character. Acts 8:5–8 concerns a city in Samaria that had a specific personality and character which, through the influence of Philip's hands–on ministry, was transformed in a positive way. Cities can undergo transformational change depending on the type of ministry that takes place there on the part of the people of God.

I have had the privilege of visiting Hungary on a number of occasions, working with ministry leadership in that land as well as with leaders from other nations in Eastern Europe. If we were to evaluate the gifting of Hungary as a nation, the list is numerous. In speaking with leaders and in researching both past and present history, it is clearly a land full of hospitality, giving and generosity. Its people are always ready to help others in time of need. Its citizens have created inventions that have benefited the globe. Many parts of Hungary reveal the beauty of art and architecture in that land. A quick visit to Heroes' Square

When a nation has its boundary lines shifted or changed, inevitably this has an effect upon the developing life of the people within that nation.

in Budapest reveals the strength and determination of the people to survive the many challenges they have had over the years. The Danube River is well known to romantics and historians! Both tourism and commercial river traffic indicate this river is indeed a meeting place for other nations.

However, a careful look at the history of the land also reveals a number of prevailing strongholds. Some of the characteristics of these strongholds include envy, suspicion, a sense of division and a legacy of other nations taking advantage of Hungary. As a nation, Hungary has experienced a theft of her heritage, her inheritance, her land and her people. Invasions by the Mongols, Turks and Communists have left an ongoing influence. Negative spiritual issues have continued to exist there over many years. It is not an easy place for effective evangelism. One prominent national symbol is the *Turul*, a mythical bird–like creature representing power, strength, and ability which is still used today on the coat of arms of the Hungarian army and the office of national security. It is clearly based upon shamanistic folklore.

When a nation has its boundary lines shifted or changed, inevitably this has an effect upon the developing life of the people within that nation. Memories of the past cannot easily be overlooked or quickly forgotten. Land and people removed from a nation have serious consequences. The whole subject of "stolen land" is a painful issue for many first nation groups around the world. Many treaties and agreements were entered into between First Nations people groups and those who settled on their land. Most of these treaties have been broken or betrayed, such as we find in the history of North America. Even while this book is being written, governments, including the Canadian government have been working with various First Nations representatives in trying to determine where gross error has occurred historically, how this can be acknowledged, and to what degree any suitable restitution may be feasible.

To cite just one of many such examples, when Great Britain and the United States established a boundary line between Maine and New Brunswick in 1842, the Passamaquoddy people were not consulted. Such a lack of negotiation is typical of many agreements made with aboriginal peoples. As a result, Passamaquoddy families were separated and traditional territory seized. From their perspective, this was a major breach in their physical and spiritual history. It resulted in commercial profiteering by other people and their own exploitation as a unique people group. From their viewpoint, they had occupied a particular watershed region for at least 600 generations, but were then compelled to live under an imposed boundary line established approximately 200 years ago. Wikipedia and other websites explain their perspective: "The newcomers violate treaties with Passamaquoddy, they take our land, pollute our waters, deplete our food source, and make laws (in violation of treaties) that restrict our hunting, fishing, travel and trade within our homeland. Our way of life in endangered."[2]

No matter how this is justified, when the boundary line is stolen or changed, it does have an effect upon the people living within that area. History is replete with ongoing examples of injustices that occur when covenants and agreements are broken and the resident people are forced to endure the consequences.

RESTORING GOD'S BOUNDARY LINES

God's template for a nation is similar to that of a city, a business, a church or even that of an individual. However, most books written concerning the boundaries God establishes for His people are done so on a relational basis, without the connection between the physical and the spiritual. Over the years, we have had the privilege of working with cities, territories and businesses in recognizing boundary lines and boundary stones which were established by God but, for one reason or another, were either forfeited or neglected—or even stolen.

James (his real name changed in order to protect his identity) is the CEO and President of Abundant Grain Association. It includes active farming as well as the exporting of various types of seed and grain to at least 70 nations in the global arena. All the major religious systems in the world are represented within these countries. Some of these nations are under Hindu, Islamic and Buddhist influences. James and his company are based in a strategic agricultural area in North America.

Prior to our first meeting with James, he was enjoying a relatively successful farming and seed business, but was aware of limitations and issues that God seemed to be asking him to address. Following our initial time of ministry with him on the land, his productivity doubled in some cases and went from average to high quality in its yield. To the degree that he incorporated prayer and hands–on ministry upon the land as a key component of his business, it continued to expand in both quantity and influence both at home and abroad. The principles utilized for praying upon land and the stewarding of land are outlined clearly in my books, *Releasing Heaven on Earth*[3] and *Transformed! People – Cities – Nations.*[4]

In due course James and his company began to extend their boundary lines under the direction of the Lord. They purchased two properties a significant distance from his home base. However with the purchase of these new properties, certain challenges also developed, including certain staff difficulties. Former management and remaining employees had a minimum sense of responsibility in caring for the upkeep of the facilities. The former ownership and stewardship had ongoing influence on these new properties and upon the land itself, which consequently had significant effects upon its present circumstances and productivity. Furthermore, people in the area felt they were entitled to enter the premises with their own agendas.

When we met with James we visited both properties on various occasions and we asked him some candid questions concerning the boundary lines of both properties. It was quite obvious there was a significant amount of old machinery and unusable items on both properties. After these were correctly surveyed, we learned that the land they had purchased actually infringed on adjacent property belonging to a railroad company. In other words, they had unwittingly extended their borders ***beyond their legal and spiritual ownership.*** This began to account for the confusion and lack of productivity and stability within these new properties. The issues on the land and in the spirit realm on these adjacent properties had now been inherited by James! In other words, **they had been entering into battles that were not theirs to fight!**

Issues that they had inherited from their previous owners were clearly hindering the business and productivity. Upon investigation, words had been spoken and agreements had been made based on sleight–of–hand that broke covenants and gave the right of access for the enemy and his influence. Once purchased legally from the railroad company, the land in both centers was then prayed over and staked as outlined in Isaiah 54:2–4. Several of the Scriptures referred to earlier in this book concerning boundary lines and boundary stones were adhered to and implemented utilizing the correct posture of forgiveness and reconciliation and a renouncing of old ways upon these areas of land. This was followed by prayer for God's healing to be released and implemented. As they prayed for the land, life was spoken into the ground (Jeremiah 22:29), and the expectancy of new life and productivity was released. Issues, including inventory and ownership connected to the previous owners and their respective soul ties, were thoroughly prayed through with an expectation that God wanted to do something new in a corporate sense in these newly acquired areas of business.

Consequently, processing and sales doubled at the newly purchased properties with a significant shift in the spiritual atmosphere. Former employees who held on to the 'old ways' resigned. New employees have now been added to the company which has created a much better atmosphere in the overall business. Bumper crops have occurred with both seeds and yields in the high range. Farmers in the respective areas have prospered. As we will see shortly, when the people of God enter into a proper understanding of their covenant relationship with Him, they then become a template for the rest of the area in order that the eyes of the people are opened to see the goodness of the Lord. This is a very important and powerful principle in any form of marketplace stewardship within the life of a nation, a city, a local business and a church. To the degree that issues are addressed in the spirit realm, there will be a cause–and–effect shift taking place on the physical realm, even upon the productivity of the land. We have witnessed this principle on hundreds of occasions in various parts of the world.

When boundary lines and boundary stones have been moved, shifted, neglected or even stolen, this has a significant effect upon any form of productivity taking place in that area. When God asks us to extend His influence by enabling us to access and own new territory, then He gives to us the proper protocol and directions for bringing this to pass, as outlined in Scripture. Upon the purchase of their new properties, The Abundant Grain Association was out of alignment with their legal boundaries and some of their purchased equipment was on adjacent land not under their ownership. Once they brought themselves within God's boundary lines, then they were no longer under the impact of spiritual and physical trespassing. Their company had been 'out of bounds' and they suffered the consequences. But when addressed correctly, everything came into alignment both relationally and within the business realm.

The company as a whole had been incorrectly informed concerning the land purchase. The importance of knowing their legal boundaries became of paramount importance in order to address the spiritual issues accordingly. What has happened since then has been an amazing testimony. James and his company are well known for the quality and integrity of their productivity in many nations around the world. They have indeed become a global corporation. Even when in countries which are under Islamic and Buddhist influence, James has been given considerable access to the churches. He is known as a Christian of integrity since his product and business are based upon integrity. This has become his ongoing experience in many different parts of the world. He is quick to testify that the blessings as outlined in Deuteronomy 28:1–14 and Leviticus 26:1–13 are indeed accurate. Leviticus 26:11–13 reveals a profound blessing from God Himself— *"I will put my dwelling place among you, and I will not abhor you. I will walk among you and be your God, and you will be my people. I am the Lord your God, who brought you out of Egypt so that you would no longer be slaves to the Egyptians; I broke the bars of your yoke and enabled you to walk with heads held high."*

In 2 Chronicles 29 when Hezekiah was called to bring healing to the land due to the generations of defilement and idolatry, he undertook a very specific strategy which in a short period of time yielded a significant change within and upon the land. 2 Chronicles 29:36 states, *"Hezekiah and all the people rejoiced at what God had brought about for his people, because it was done so quickly."* A significant shift took place upon the land and within the atmosphere in the area. James said to me that, in his case, he believes this is the evidence of transformation and healing upon the land since it has brought gladness to the communities in which new acquisitions had been made. There has been a significant change in the attitude of the people in both areas towards his company. It is also worthy of note that upon acquiring these new properties, further research revealed that these properties were adjacent to original property owned by his father. Godly inheritance is of importance to the Lord!

In those earlier years, there had been fairly significant Freemasonic influence, which resulted in other issues that negatively impacted the land and the business. It was as if God was now reordering and realigning things into what He had originally wanted for James and the legacy of his seed and his company. Indeed, it is all about "nurturing" one's legacy given by the Lord. In James' own words to me, he recognizes that having the correct "earned authority" is essential for understanding God's boundary lines, and knowing how to steward them and also how and when to extend them.

One other example to cite as an illustration of addressing one's boundary lines involves two people known as John and Diane. John and Diane own a significant storage facility in the USA that they developed as part of their stewardship responsibility before the Lord, both as a legacy for their family and also as a means of financing their own ministry within the global arena. Upon completing the purchase of their new property and, in due course after establishing this large storage facility, they began to experience a number of hindrances within their productivity. It was as if the fruit of their labor was continually stolen or forfeited. Their facility was only half full and they needed a higher clientele not only to pay the bills, but also to supplement and facilitate their marketplace ministry. When we were asked to meet with them and to pray over their property, we encouraged them to undertake some research upon the land. In due course it was revealed there had been aboriginal bloodshed upon this land. Also it had been used for the training of young troops before they were sent overseas to war. Clearly, there had been all forms of trauma on this land which had impacted the spirit realm and now was impacting its productivity.

John and Diane were now the legal as well as spiritual owners of this land, and we were invited to join them, thus coming under legal authority for our time of prayer. After addressing the issues of trauma through confession, forgiveness, renunciation and speaking healing onto the land, the boundary areas were staked and prayed over. The land was also dedicated for God's purposes to be released. In a relatively short time, the occupancy was full with a 20%–30% waiting list. New clients would come sometimes from other areas bypassing other storage facilities en route. When asked why they did this, they commented how they felt secure when on John and Diane's property and also felt their belongings would be secure under their care!

When order is restored and disorder is addressed, then health and healing can be anticipated and experienced for an entire community and for the overall productivity of that land.

As with any business, there is a need to steward what God gives us. Despite recession and occasional times when clients leave, normally there is a full clientele that meets both the bills and staff expenses as well as releasing John and Diane for the ministry to which God has called them. Again, this was a matter of dealing with boundary lines as well as addressing areas neglected over the years. These issues that had been ignored allowed for various forms of both spiritual, physical and economic vulnerability and violation to take place, which consequently affected all forms of productivity on the land.

These two examples of James, John and Diane and their respective companies describe the template we have used in watching cities—their inhabitants and institutions—coming into alignment with God's purposes. At times it is hard to distinguish boundary lines because of all the shifts and moves that take place within present day society. But when we seek the counsel of the Lord and inquire of Him upon this matter, He gives clarity and insight and direction—along with the necessary correction. When order is restored and disorder is addressed, then health and healing can be anticipated and experienced for an entire community, for the inhabitants of the land and for the overall productivity of that land. This is the importance of understanding boundary lines and boundary stones from God's perspective.

---

1. *Releasing Heaven on Earth* Author: Alistair P Petrie – Republished July 2008 – Sovereign World Ltd. ISBN 97818 52404 819
2. Further information concerning the Passamaquoddy Tribe is available on various research websites – www.wikipedia.org/wiki/Passamaquoddy_people http://www.passamaquoddy.com
3. *Releasing Heaven on Earth* Author: Alistair P Petrie – Republished July 2008 – Sovereign World Ltd. ISBN 97818 52404 819
4. *Transformed! People – Cities – Nations* Author: Alistair P Petrie – Republished July 2008 – Sovereign World Ltd. ISBN 97818 52404 826

6

ACCESSING CITIES and Nations

In Ruth 1:19 we are told Ruth and Naomi have chosen to stay together and to enter their destiny by travelling to Bethlehem. We read these arresting words— *"When they arrived in Bethlehem, the whole town was stirred because of them, and the women exclaimed, 'Can this be Naomi?'"* (Ruth 1:19) As Jesus neared His destiny in Jerusalem, He enters the city on a donkey and we are told in Matthew 21:10 that *"When Jesus entered Jerusalem, the whole city was stirred..."* When we enter our destiny that God has prepared for us, even entire cities will be stirred to attention! In other words, we are giving a wake–up call to both the spiritual realm as well as the physical realm that we are there on the Lord's business on His terms.

The stirring of a city does not necessarily mean everything is positive and there are no challenges...instead, it means that we are there under God's direction and working with a Godly authority that will create a wake–up call within the city. In order for a city or a nation to undergo this type of "stirring", it is important that we know how to access the area correctly. There are various teachings that exist today giving some degree of insight as to how to pray into cities and nations in order that they submit to the purposes of God. The proof in the pudding, of course, will be the fruit that comes from such efforts. This will determine the effectiveness of any type of strategy.

Over the years we have determined that every city and nation has distinct access points which, when, properly researched and understood, give insight as to the real issues that need to be addressed. Every strategy is different based on the conditions that exist within each area.

UNDERSTANDING ACCESS POINTS

The **initial access point** is almost always **the Church** depending on what form it may take in any particular area. We have always found that the Church is a "litmus test" that enables us to understand what exactly is happening in the city or on the land. In other words, whatever problems or challenges the Church is facing also represents what is happening in the wider area. It is as if God gives the Church the initial insight and, when issues are prayed and worked through correctly, then the Church becomes a fundamental catalyst in releasing an authentic hands–on ministry. This results in breakthrough and transformation. When referring to the Church, we are looking both at the "four walled church" as well as the Church in the marketplace. When the issues that need to be addressed are repaired, healed and made whole, then the Church becomes an authentic instrument of change for the larger area.

The **second access point** is the **legal arena**. This is composed of the police force in whatever form it may exist, lawyers, judges—anything, in fact, which reflects the law of the land. We are looking to see what areas of sin, sleight of hand, or corruption may have existed there over the years. Then, through the process of locating those who have legitimate earned authority in those areas and who are therefore able to undertake the necessary process of identificational repentance, the issues in that access point are addressed and healed. This in turn becomes a strategic prophetic voice and reference point for the whole of the legal arena in that area.

The **third access point** is the **political arena**. Whatever goes on in politics—whether at a federal, regional, or local level—from the past or in the present, continues to have an ongoing effect on life and work in that area. Once people are identified who can effectively stand in the gap within this third access point, we are then provided with a significant influence that can shape the manner in which politics can be a catalyst for the purposes of God.

The **fourth area** that we research concerns **education** from the preschool level to the post–secondary. This involves students, teachers and the educational system as a whole. It also affects school boards that legislate curricula taught within school systems and so decide whether reference to God is acceptable or not. This is an area of significant lobbying in this day and age. One of the sayings of the Jesuits used to be: "Give me the child until he is seven, and I will give you the man." The Barna Research Group[1] has indicated that worldviews tend to be firmly in place by the time a person is 13 years old (Barna Research Group 2009).

The **fifth access** point involves the area of **industry, trade and commerce**. This is, of course, a highly strategic part of any city and nation. Normally it will represent part of the unique redemptive gifting in any particular location. When business personnel are able to pray with Godly earned authority in their respective areas of influence and function, this will have a profound effect upon the life and destiny of that place.

The **sixth access point** occurs when radio, television, newspapers and sports all combine to form a **public media sphere of influence**. This can readily shift a city's perspective concerning God and His plan for that city and nation. Hardly a day goes by in this day and age in which there is not some degree of shaking going on in virtually every city around the world. Usually news media highlights each in its own different way. When Godly communication takes place through those who have hands–on experience, again this has enormous influence in opening up the eyes of a city to the reality of what God may be saying.

The **seventh access point** involves the area of **the medical**: medical personnel, all forms of health practitioners, clinics and hospitals as well as fire and ambulatory services. So often it is the medical personnel who are aware of the issues taking place before they are readily communicated to the general public. When people in this area of responsibility are working within their boundary lines, utilizing earned authority under the direction of the Lord, they then become a significant catalyst of change for God's purposes.

The **eighth access point** is not always found in every city but its existence influences almost every nation in the world. It is the area of **armed forces**. These personnel, when living and working in a localized area, can import all forms of influence both negative and positive depending on their personal circumstances and the circumstances of their office and former locations of duty. However, once they encounter and participate in a community experiencing authentic Kingdom transformation, they can also become effective catalysts of change to the areas where they are sent.

When these various access points work together under the direction of those who are leading the city and the nation, then both the doors and the gates of cities and nations can be opened up to the purposes of God. These are areas that represent human culture, and can become conduits of Godly culture through the life and work of the people of God in the city. When they stand in the gap and identify the issues that have to be addressed from God's perspective, and restore boundary lines and boundary stones, address areas of deception, learn to read the signs of the times and ask why God may be shaking their respective cities and nations, then they are able to pray in the purposes of God and release His redemptive change accordingly. It is not simply a matter of "declaring" change since without due diligence, no amount of declaring will result in anything lasting. One popular teaching suggests that each of these areas has a "spiritual mountain" that must be overcome or changed. However, this in itself is debatable especially when we refer to the first access point being that of the Church. Granted, there may be a religious spirit within the Church, but if the Church is purely viewed as a mountain that has to be overcome, then we are in danger of teaching a questionable form of Dominionism in which man knows better than God.

A CHECK–LIST

Over the years as we have utilized this outline of the various access points in a city or nation, we have time and again seen significant shift and change in how God's transforming power has come to inhabit the people and the fabric of the institutions in each area.

The Church is a key component in authentic transformation. It really is and always will be the prophetic mouthpiece by which other impediments need to be addressed.

An important question we are often asked as a ministry is how we can determine if the strategy of prayer given in any particular location is sufficient for what God wants to undertake. Here is an outline of what we would describe as the "non–negotiables" that need to be examined and applied in every instance:

Ensure that there are many Scriptures being used to explain the process of praying through each of these access points. The issue of cities and nations are of paramount importance to God, and He has given many templates in both the Old and New Testaments that validate this principle.

Ensure that what is being undertaken as a strategy is in full compliance with the Word of God and does not lean into the area of extra–biblical or experiential theology. Otherwise, we become overly subjective in our approach to what is being undertaken.

We have already referred to the concern of viewing the Church as a mountain which needs to be addressed. There are serious implications in this perspective. The Church is a key component in authentic transformation circles as we have been watching now for many years. The Church really is and always will be the prophetic mouthpiece by which other impediments or "mountains" need to be addressed whether we are referring to the "four–walled church" or the "church without walls". God chooses to work in a refining and defining manner within His Church so that it exerts Kingdom influence and direction upon the rest of society. Therefore a healthy and accountable implementation of the five–fold ministry gifts needs to be stewarded wisely, especially the relationship between the Apostle and the Prophet. We need to ensure this is in place.

Ensure that the strategy being implemented for praying through the city, territory or nation is one that has been given by the Lord specifically for that area. If it is merely "imported" from another template in a different location, then it is debatable whether or not it will be relevant and effective in the new situation. Principles rarely change, but strategy almost always is based upon the contextual uniqueness and individuality of each location. The purposes of God for one place may be entirely different from that of another.

It is important to determine that the key issue of "Identificational Repentance" is being undertaken correctly. The sins of omission and commission need to be confessed accordingly, each followed with forgiveness, renunciation, reconciliation and where necessary with restitution. This involves working in the opposite spirit to that which may have affected or influenced the city adversely over many years. This is followed with the breaking of bondages, strongholds and any soul ties that may have developed. Indeed, even the issue of sister cities or the "twinning of cities" may need to be addressed. Very often different locations are twinned out of pragmatic and expeditious rationale, and most are unaware that there is also a linking which takes place in the spiritual realm. Over the years we have been involved in this ministry, time and time again we have found that when one city or nation is twinned with another, almost right away there is a significant spiritual shift in these areas. This requires diligent research and a constant inquiring of the Lord, especially if the healing of the land and God's transforming power are to be the end result.

Ensure that there is a proper understanding of **stewarding** with regard to what has been undertaken in terms of influencing all the access points of a city and a nation. If we do not guard, keep and occupy correctly, it is highly probable that any change we experience will recede. Slowly things return to the way they were before any initiative was ever undertaken. In fact, things may even become worse. This is a Biblical principle. (Matthew 12:43–45; Luke 11:24–26) It is important to have a team in place willing to steward that which has been started and to ensure it is sustained.

> It is always important we learn how to minister in the opposite spirit to that which has been familiar to the city.

Concerning corporate transformation at any level, it is essential that we ourselves go through personal transformation. This is necessary in order to have the "earned authority" and the believing expectancy that what we pray for really can come to pass. If we are simply *declaring* without addressing root issues that must be honestly addressed starting with ourselves, then we will see little, if any, lasting change. It is always important we learn how to minister in the opposite spirit to that which has been familiar to the city but which has estranged it from the purposes of God.

Understand the importance of waiting on the counsel, direction and timing of the Holy Spirit. God requires us to undertake proper research framed within strategic prayer. If indeed there are impediments in any spiritual mountains that have to be addressed, we have to know **why** they exist in the first place in order for prayer to become an effective catalyst of change. Again, we are resisting copying templates and strategies from other areas. We need to become very familiar with each individual situation and minister accordingly.

In cases when First Nations people have had past and present influence in any given location, their input and involvement is essentially non–negotiable. Determining the right representatives for each occasion is important and it becomes part of the responsibility of the leadership to ensure that the right people are standing in the right gap at the right time, and that all are of one mind and heart for the purposes of God. This will be of particular importance when going through the areas of forgiveness and repentance and even restitution concerning sinful activities in the past, as well as in the overall template of the healing of the land.

There should be at least a minimum level of authentic "hands on" research undertaken in as objective a manner as possible allowing for the unique contextual components of each area. This includes an understanding or awareness of the spiritual issues involved in cities and nations in which local – national – international and global issues are assessed and made available for proper prayer preparation and implementation. Almost everyone today is affected by the global arena in one way or another. We are watching this occur within nations such as those in Europe who are being required to respond to requests through the higher organizations such as the European Union. The trickledown effect upon cities, businesses and individuals, is almost unavoidable, and we must be able to pray accordingly and effectively.

All of this is non–negotiable. When these procedures as outlined form part of an effective prayer strategy, then the counsel, the activity and the destiny of the Lord is released. When God's boundary lines and boundary stones have been restored, then significant changes **can** take place.

BOUNDARY LINES AND PLEASANT PLACES

As Psalm 16:5–6 would indicate, when our boundary lines are secured by the Lord, then we have a delightful inheritance. Other translations refer to these boundary lines promising us a good heritage or a bountiful heritage. When considering these two verses, most commentaries will intimate that this refers to enjoying God's favor and friendship in the very area in which He has positioned us. Jeremiah 3:19 states, *"How gladly would I treat you like sons and give you a desirable land, the most beautiful inheritance of any nation..."* What is astounding about God is that He longs for His people to be established in the fullness of His inheritance that He has prepared for them. (Acts 13:19; Ephesians 1:18; 2:10; Hebrews 11:8)

We are living in an era in which the curtain is being raised and we are watching the earth being shaken at every possible level.

However, there is a deeper inference in that God does want to give to His people portion and inheritance in order for them to steward His purposes in their respective areas of responsibility. In so doing these areas will be "pleasant" and "delightful". We will experience the presence of the Lord in our midst. 2 Chronicles 7:14 promises that when we pray and seek His face and turn from our wicked ways, He hears from heaven, He forgives sin, and He heals land, but verses 15 and 16 also promise that *His* eyes and ears will be attentive to the prayers offered in that area because He chooses to have His name placed in the midst of His people who honor Him with all their hearts and seek His purposes in their lives. God loves to take delight and rejoice in the very areas where His presence is made welcome. It is within these areas of our responsibility that He gives to us what is required to release His transforming power. Jesus himself refers to us as a city set on a hill (Matthew 5:14). It is God's intention for us to reflect His light and His hope so that as people see Him at work in our lives they will give praise to God in Heaven. (Matthew 5:16)

We are living in an era in which the curtain is being raised and we are watching the earth being shaken at every possible level. This is a time of urgency, and it is a time to be asking the right questions in order to fight the right battles. It is a time in which deception is at work in our midst and we need to be able to identify it. It is a time in which God is asking us to restore His Godly boundaries in our respective areas of responsibility and influence even at the levels of cities and nations.

"BEING DILIGENT IN THESE MATTERS" (1 Timothy 4:15–16)

Paul encourages Timothy to be diligent in key matters pertaining to the work and witness of the Church. All of 1 Timothy 4 is a timely wake–up call to the Church of the 21st Century on key matters pertaining to life, ministry, Scripture and doctrine. In particular verse 16 is a salient reminder—"*Watch your life and doctrine closely. Persevere in them, because if you do, you will save both yourself and your hearers.*" The Darby Translation[2] translates verse 15— "Occupy thyself with these things..." The Good News translation[3] says to "practice these things" (v15) and "to watch yourself and watch your teaching..." (v16)

To "occupy ourselves" with all this in mind seems essential if we are going to respond correctly to God's wake–up call to His Church for a time such as this. We are His prophetic voice in society—and until the Lord returns, we have an appointed task at hand that requires our being alert and sober and responsive to the hour that is at hand. Deception is in our midst and we need to know how to respond accordingly. Yet at the same time God has given us strategic boundaries to guide and inform us—as well as to direct us, and when necessary to correct us. In so doing He has made our lot secure, and has caused our boundary lines to have fallen in sweet places, ensuring we have a delightful inheritance.

We are living in challenging times, but as we have seen, God has given us a blueprint for navigating these days of profound shift and change. It is a time in which He is challenging His people to wake up...for heaven's sake!

---

1. The Barna Group website – www.barna.org
2. From Wikipedia, *The Darby Bible*, John Nelson Darby, based on his 1890 publication *Translation of the New Testament*; www.biblegateway.com/versions/Darby–Translation–Bible

3. *Good News Translation* (GNT), 1966, 1971, 1976, American Bible Society – www.biblegateway.com ISBN 08883 40427

GLOSSARY

Dominion Theology

At times also referred to as Kingdom Theology, this term is used to describe the commission of the Church to bring the entire world under the dominion and influence of Christianity before the Return of Jesus Christ. Based on the understanding that God originally gave dominion to man to have dominion over the earth, this was lost due to the Fall of Adam and Eve, but then returned to the Church following Christ's victory on the Cross. The belief is that the Lord will return once the Church has fulfilled this mandate.

Experiential Theology

Positively, it is a theology which explains how the doctrines of Scripture become an experiential and living reality in the hearts and lives of believers. Negatively, it can lead to an experience trumping Scripture and redefining doctrine, or even developing new doctrine from an experience that may be beyond the boundaries of Scripture, therefore leading towards a modern form of Gnosticism.

Gnosticism

This term is derived from the Greek word "gnosis" which means knowledge. There were groups in the Early Church that said salvation could only be received through a special or secret or higher knowledge—and not necessarily limited to what was contained in Scripture. This type of gnostic belief was most probably prevalent before Christianity in which a mindset of dualism separated the spiritual and material worlds with God being too pure to be involved with material issues. It was and still is a serious heresy since in essence it denies the necessity of the Incarnation and Atonement.

Postmodernism Gnosticism

This is a philosophical stance which claims that it is essentially impossible to make grand statements—meta–narratives—about the structures of society or about historic causation, since everything we perceive, express and interpret is influenced by our gender, class and culture; knowledge is partial and situated, and no one interpretation is superior to another.

Extra Biblical

This term can be used to describe research that is undertaken to view history and culture when interpreting Scripture. It can also be a description of ministry that is based purely on subjective experience. The danger is when it replaces inspired Scripture and becomes in itself a definitive or even final authority. Biblical boundaries therefore can be easily suggestive rather than directive and corrective.

Post–millennialism

This is an interpretation of end–times theology based on Revelation 20 which views the second coming of Jesus Christ as occurring after the millennium or thousand year reign of Christ upon earth, which in some postmillennial circles would say has already begun. This teaching often is contained within Dominion Theology. While this viewpoint can be somewhat varied, most proponents would hold the view that the forces of Satan and his kingdom will be increasingly defeated as the expansion of the Kingdom of God increases upon earth, that things are getting better, and which ultimately will usher in the Return of Christ.

Praxis

A term that describes a process by which a lesson, skill or discipline operates or is practiced within a variety of circles, including spiritual, political and educational. It can readily be associated in describing a form of liturgy as expressed through a church denomination.

Earned Authority

This is a term that explains the Christian's personal journey of Sanctification in which the message and authority of the Cross is applied at personal level in the life of the believer. Knowing the victory of Christ in theory is one thing, but going through the process of activating and applying the promises of Scripture especially in areas of great vulnerability and temptation is quite another. It is having the understanding that Jesus also has been tempted in every way known to humanity (Hebrews 2:18; 4:15) yet has overcome the temptation and through activating this victory of Christ, we can appropriate His promises. Thus, in turn, enables His people to minister more effectively to those also going through similar areas of vulnerability since such people now have an "earned authority" in that specific area of ministry.

Cloaking Device

For the purpose of this book, cloaking is a term is based on a fictional technology used within the Star Trek television series in which space craft could actually be present yet at the same time remain hidden from their adversaries. In many of the episodes, personnel would perceive distortion without accurately determining what was really present.

Antinomianism

Within historic Christian circles following the Protestant Reformation, various forms of Antinomianism—anti (against) nomos (law)—have appeared with the belief that since the Gospel demonstrates the grace of God, then moral law is of little or any significance, since only faith is necessary for salvation. On–going forgiveness of sin is therefore not necessarily required, if everything is already forgiven under the Cross. The issue of consequences for one's sins as a Christian therefore become minimalized.

Fantasy Thinking

For the purpose of this book, this term is derived from a form of thinking rooted in analytical psychology that promotes prayer essentially based on fantasy or unreality. It is also founded upon emotion or intuition and is without logical or moral constraints. At times it comes from one's soulishness and hopefulness but is re–interpreted as a definitive Word from the Lord without proper testing from the Word of God.

ABOUT THE AUTHOR

For many years in both the United Kingdom and Canada, Alistair served as senior pastor in diverse city church settings. With that experience and his earlier years spent in professional broadcasting, he now serves as the Executive Director of Partnership Ministries, a global ministry that teaches the principles and relevance of the Gospel and its relationship to the Marketplace. Partnership Ministries is positioned as a ministry for the 21st Century Church and combines prayer and research in order to prepare Communities, Cities, Nations and the Marketplace for lasting revival, authentic transformation and the release of Kingdom culture. In doing so, Alistair consults regularly with church, business, and business leaders helping them in applying the principles of Transformation in their workplace environment—and explains how this releases cities and nations into their respective destinies.

Alistair travels extensively to many nations researching and teaching these transformation principles, and on occasion teaches a one–week Marketplace School. Obtaining his Doctorate through Fuller Seminary, he has been a guest lecturer at several academic settings and Schools of Ministry. As well as being an international speaker, he is the author of several books, and along with his ministry team has produced an informative DVD teaching series. He is married to Marie and along with their two sons, Mike and Richard, their entire family serve the wider church and the Marketplace in the global arena.

Partnership Ministries

www.partnershipministries.org